Improving Children's Mental Health
Through Parent Empowerment

Edited by Peter S. Jensen ■ *Kimberly Eaton Hoagwood*

Improving Children's Mental Health Through Parent Empowerment

A Guide to Assisting Families

UNIVERSITY PRESS

2008

OXFORD
UNIVERSITY PRESS

Oxford University Press, Inc., publishes works that further
Oxford University's objective of excellence
in research, scholarship, and education.

Oxford   New York

Auckland   Cape Town   Dar es Salaam   Hong Kong   Karachi
Kuala Lumpur   Madrid   Melbourne   Mexico City   Nairobi
New Delhi   Shanghai   Taipei   Toronto

With offices in
Argentina   Austria   Brazil   Chile   Czech Republic   France   Greece
Guatemala   Hungary   Italy   Japan   Poland   Portugal   Singapore
South Korea   Switzerland   Thailand   Turkey   Ukraine   Vietnam

Copyright © 2008 by Oxford University Press, Inc.

Published by Oxford University Press, Inc.
198 Madison Avenue, New York, New York 10016
www.oup.com

Oxford is a registered trademark of Oxford University Press

Library of Congress Cataloging-in-Publication Data
Improving children's mental health through parent empowerment : a guide to assisting families /
edited by Peter S. Jensen, Kimberly Eaton Hoagwood.
p. cm.
Includes bibliographical references and index.
ISBN: 978-0-19-532090-9
1. Child mental health services. 2. Parents of mentally ill children—Counseling of.
3. Counselors—Training of. 4. Parent-student counselor relationships. I. Jensen, Peter S.
II. Hoagwood, Kimberly.
RJ500.I49 2008 618.92'89—dc22   2007045740

9 8 7 6 5 4 3 2 1

Printed in the United States of America
on acid-free paper

Contents

Part I

Building a Strong Foundation for Working With Parents

Part II

Assisting Parents in Navigating the Mental Health System

Contributors

The REACH Institute

Peter S. Jensen, M.D., director and president

Columbia University

Kimberly Eaton Hoagwood, Ph.D., professor of clinical psychology (in psychiatry) in the division of services and policy research

Polly Gipson, former research assistant, parent empowerment program

Lisa Hunter Romanelli, Ph.D., director, evidence based school intervention programs and assistant professor, clinical psychology (in psychiatry)

Serene Olin, Ph.D., director of school parent empowerment programs, and instructor, clinical psychology in the division of services and policy research

Belinda Ramos, M.A., director of parent empowerment training

James Rodriquez, Ph.D., director, parent empowerment programs, and instructor, clinical psychology (in psychiatry)

Mental Health Association of New York City

Geraldine Burton, FDC, parent advocate

Adam Stein, Ph.D., consultant, independent practice. Former clinical consultant, Mental Health Association of NYC, and senior consultant, parent empowerment programs

RueZalia Watkins, education services specialist, Mental Health Association of NYC

Preface

The idea for this book was born at the same time as each of our children. It arose directly from our experiences first and foremost as parents, then as mental health consumers for our children, and then as citizens impatient with the status quo and committed to making a difference in children's lives.

One of us (KEH) is a parent of a daughter who as a teenager came close to death twice. Her life was saved because of organ transplantation (and the generosity of anonymous parents who lost their own child). However, she had initial struggles with her physical health in the time preceding her second successful transplant. She also experienced—and continues to struggle with—mental health challenges, such as recurrent depression and panic disorder. She is now a youth advocate. Through her experiences with both the health and the mental health systems, I saw firsthand how parents could become a critical link in the chain of their child's health care. I saw how some health care professionals welcomed the chance to fully engage parents in the decision process, to share information, and to deal them in. I saw others who shunned parents altogether, shutting them out of critical decisions involving their child. I saw how the combination of parents and professionals working together in partnership—as a team—to make what were sometimes life-and-death decisions could be a powerful force shaping in profound ways the future of their children's lives.

One of us (GS) has a daughter who was diagnosed with bipolar disorder and hospitalized at the age of 12. She is now 21 and attending college. She has traveled abroad, she has lived on an entirely different coast than her family, and she has a job that she loves. During the height of her illness, I learned how powerless parents feel as they watch their children's lives drastically change. Even having spent my whole professional life working in the mental health field, I was at a loss to find the best services for her. And though I consulted many professionals, the information and support I received from talking to other parents of children with similar challenges was what helped me see the light at the end of this long, dark tunnel. That's when I learned firsthand the importance of putting the tools in the hands of parents—information about medication and treatment, schooling options, and the know-how to navigate the many systems of care that affect a child's life. I also learned that there is another element beyond getting the information that is equally important: the emotional support I received from these parents. They had cried the same tears and had experienced the same sense of loss and shattered dreams and came out stronger for it, as did their children. Parents gave me the information and strength I needed to help my child when she needed it the most. Having gone through that experience, I realized that I was now uniquely equipped not only to empower other parents in the same way but also to make a contribution to the field in which I had dedicated my career. Today there is a strong and ever-growing movement of parents helping other parents. One by one, we help each other, but together we form a powerful force on behalf of our own children and all children whose lives are affected by mental illness.

And for one of us (PSJ), it was only by being "hit upside the head" by families that I came to understand the essential role that experienced parents "who have been there" must play in assisting parents and families newly entering and struggling with the mental health system. Trained in the "olden days," I was essentially taught that parents were usually "the problem" and virtually never the solution. My views and, essentially, my entire professional identity began to change after I came to work for the federal government at the National Institute of Mental Health in 1989. Beginning that fall, I attended several meetings where I began to hear firsthand from parents and families about the obstacles and barriers they encountered when attempting to get their children necessary assistance in "the system." I was appalled to realize that, all too often, it was the attitudes and beliefs of mental health "professionals" such as myself that added to the already heavy burdens of stigma on these families. And, in fact, I could recall instances in my own career where instead of proactively helping a given family, I was subtly withholding my assistance but not withholding judgments. Since 1989, parents and families have been and remain my best teachers. This book is a small attempt to give back what I have been given.

This book is written by parents and for parents who help other parents. It is written to help parents become actively engaged in their child's mental health care. It is written to help parents become empowered to take an active role in obtaining high-quality services for their children, to become knowledgeable consumers about mental health treatments, and to become skilled in working effectively with other parents who struggle to get help for their children.

This book arose through discussions among parent advocates with the Mental Health Association of New York City, among many committed parents across the country, among New York's mental health policymakers and advocates, and among researchers. Each, from their vantage point, sought to improve the mental health system, to make it more responsive to parents' expertise, and to strengthen the potential to form active partnerships on behalf of children. It began as a series of highly charged and intellectually robust discussions. It matured through careful scientific review of the knowledge base on children's mental health and on family involvement, support, and engagement. It has emerged not as a product but as a process—one that is centered on supporting parents who work with other parents to build strong partnerships with the ultimate aim of improving mental health services for children.

So many committed people have contributed to this effort that it is with some trepidation that we begin our thanks. These individuals have shared their personal stories, their scientific work, their perspectives, and, most important, their hearts and minds. This book could not have taken shape without each and everyone. We wish to thank them all deeply.

Kimberly Eaton Hoagwood
Giselle Stolper
Peter S. Jensen

Acknowledgments

The editors and authors wish to acknowledge the special contributions of multiple persons who participated in the preparation, review, and editing of the manuscript, as it has been worked, reworked, and refined over a 6-year process, including Meghan Tomb, Maura Crowe, Noa Saka, Wanda Greene, Clara Augusta, Nicole McDonald, Bernadine Meeks, Sonya Omosanya, Maria Sostre-Rivera, Adam Stein, PhD, and Priscilla Shorter.

In addition, special thanks are due to Giselle Stolper of the New York City Mental Health Association and Harold Koplewicz of the New York University Child Study Center, who with the editors initially conceived of the need for such a manual and training resource. During the preparation of earlier versions of the manual, Polly Gipson, Andrea Anushko, Joanna Legerski, and Dorian Traube were key in preparing first drafts, integrating research information into the manual, and gathering the ongoing input of expert parents in order to ensure that the materials were scientifically accurate as well as user and family friendly.

Mary McKay and Leonard Bickman both contributed generously from their own research materials and vast experience. In addition, expert parents and mental health professionals applied the manuals within their own settings and offer outstanding input to improving these materials throughout the process, including Sherilin Rowley and Kristina Hindert from LINCS, Salt Lake City, Utah; Ross Andelman and Susan Waters from Contra-Costa Health Services, Contra-Costa County, California; Bruno Anthony and Laura Foster from the Maryland Center for Attention and Developmental Disorders; and Margo Levy, Carolyn Buyse, Sacha Inglis, and Dori Kaplan from District 75, New York City Department of Education. In addition, multiple persons, too numerous to mention, from various levels of the New York Office of Mental Health and New York state family support agencies provided ongoing support and input (and, often, corrective feedback!) to these materials.

Finally, the editors offer a special thanks to Belinda Ramos (Columbia University) and Julia TerMaat (Oxford University Press), who patiently have labored with the entire group to see the process through its final stages and into print.

Generous support for this project was provided by the Center for the Advancement of Children's Mental Health and various city, federal, and private grants to the two editors.

Improving Children's Mental Health Through Parent Empowerment

Introduction and Background Information

Belinda Ramos

Geraldine Burton

Kimberly Eaton Hoagwood

Peter Jensen

This guide is intended to provide parent advisors with a comprehensive tool for improving their professional effectiveness. It is a resource for parents in helping and empowering other parents to learn how to get their children's mental health needs met. There are many different terms used to describe parent-to-parent support. These include parent or family advocate, advisor, coordinator, support specialist, liaison, mentor, and coach, among others. In this book, we will use the term "parent advisor," but we recognize that there are many different functions and roles that describe the work of families who help other families. It is also recognized that individuals (other than biological parents) may assume the responsibilities for the care of children. Throughout this guide, the term "parent" is broadly used to describe any caregiver who takes on the role of parenting children. Ideally, this guide provides parent advisors essential background and knowledge for use within a face-to-face, sustained training program. However, it has also been designed as a stand-alone reference for circumstances in which formal hands-on training is not available.

This resource is for parent advisors who would like to do the following:

- Enhance their skills in engaging and empowering families of children with mental health needs
- Increase their knowledge of mental disorders, treatments, and services
- Improve their understanding about the roles, responsibilities, and opportunities that can be experienced as a parent advisor

Development of This Guide

This guide is the result of the hard work and close collaboration of parents, mental health professionals, and university researchers from New York, California, Maryland, Tennessee, and Utah. In 2000, a group of parent advisors from the Mental Health Association (MHA) in New York City realized that there was a tremendous need for better training and support for themselves as well as for the many parent advisors working across the country. The MHA parent advisors joined forces with researchers at Columbia University's Center for the Advancement of Children's Mental Health (CACMH) in New York City to develop a training and support program that would address this need. Both CACMH and MHA parent advisors developed the current guide, drawing from the work of Drs. Leonard Bickman and Craig Ann Heflinger (Bickman, Heflinger, Northrup, Sonnichsen, & Schilling, 1998; Heflinger, Bickman, Northrup, & Sonnichsen, 1997). Bickman and Heflinger developed a parent empowerment intervention for families in the armed forces at Fort Bragg specifically for parents of children with mental health needs and delivered by mental health professionals.

A series of activities was initiated to develop our program. We first conducted a thorough review of the scientific literature to see whether other programs for parent advisors had been developed or tested. Although the Bickman–Heflinger program had been developed for delivery by mental health professionals, we were surprised to find no program specifically designed for delivery by *parent advisors* working with families. We thus determined that if we were to adequately assist parent advisors working with all types of families, a new manual and accompanying training materials would be needed.

Training materials were developed with a group of highly experienced parent advisors in New York City and then tested with many different groups of parent advisors in other cities and rural areas across New York and other states. Throughout this process, parent advisors have shaped and guided the development of this guide. All the materials incorporated have gone through an extensive testing and revision process spearheaded by parents and parent advisors.

From this hands-on experience, we identified a need for a separate guide addressing parent advisors directly. This resource would include much of the critical information that parent advisors need to know. With such a guide available, parent advisors would be able to draw on it as a useful standing reference before, during, and after intensive face-to-face training.

Parent Empowerment Framework

Our approach to the parent empowerment program as employed in this guide draws from two sets of knowledge: practical expertise from the parent support field and scientific studies that have identified effective strategies that, applied to families, could improve their active involvement and engagement in services. This includes studies of family empowerment processes and strategies (Bickman et al., 1998; Heflinger et al., 1997; Taub, Tighe, & Burchard, 2001), studies of engagement strategies (McKay & Bannon, 2004; Santisteban et al., 1996), and studies of family support (Fristad, Goldberg-Arnold, & Gavazzi, 2003; Ruffolo, 1998).

We believe that the merger of the knowledge gained from the day-to-day experiences of parent support work with sound scientific theory provides a good foundation for training parent advisors. The principles of parent support that guide this book were derived from discussions with key national leaders in family advocacy and support—including Trina and David Osher, Eric Bruns, and Roy Menninger—who were convened by Jane Adams, director of Kansas Keys, in 2006. At this meeting, the following principles were identified as cornerstones of parent support:

1. Parent support is individualized and tailored to the specific needs of parents and families. Parent support demonstrates a willingness to continuously assess families' needs and incorporate this information into a flexible plan that meets families "where they are at."
2. Parent support facilitates linkages of parents to agencies, services, and other families, often through a parent advisor who can function as a trusted intermediary who also "has been there" and has faced many of the same challenges.
3. Parent support is respectful and culturally competent. Appropriate parent support is nonjudgmental and encourages expression of families' ideas, preferences, and decisions while acknowledging families' struggles, efforts, and successes.
4. Parent support builds skill and helps families create a safe environment that fosters growth and empowerment. Parents develop as competent service consumers through hands-on training, role modeling and mentorship, and other skill-building activities.
5. Parent support increases parents' knowledge by providing up-to-date information about effective interventions, local resources, and referrals. It helps them make informed decisions about their child's service needs.
6. Parent support is engaging. Parent support actively partners with families to meaningfully involve them in programs and services.

7. Parent support problem solves. Optimal parent support focuses on needs and solutions by identifying successes of the past and options for continued success.
8. Parent support focuses on outcomes and success and is goal oriented. It uses high-quality evaluation methods to actively monitor the extent to which it is really useful to parents and families in achieving their goals and improving children's outcomes.
9. Parent support broadens horizons. Effective parent support expands the possibilities for parental involvement at multiples levels (from their own community level to the policy level) and cultivates a community of peer support.
10. Parent support promotes advocacy. Effective parent support informs policymakers and providers as part of a large advocacy community.

Importantly, these principles form an ethical grounding for supporting families. It is these principles that create the basis for this guide. In addition to these principles, however, decades of research on behavior change have identified a set of factors that lead individuals to change their behavior (Ajzen & Fishbein, 1981; Jaccard, 1975; Jaccard, Dodge, & Dittus, 2002; Jaccard, Litardo, & Wan, 1999).

An empowered parent is one who engages in a process of behavior change, propelled by knowledge, skills, and a sense of agency to advocate effectively on behalf of his or her child. Because the role of parent advisors often involves assisting parents to become active agents of change on behalf of their children, these behavior change factors are important to understand. According to literally hundreds of studies (see review by Fishbein et al., 2001) on the process of change, for an individual to change, he or she must have the following:

1. Knowledge about the expected behavior and skills to apply that knowledge
2. Attitudes and beliefs that indicate readiness and interest to engage in a behavior
3. Rehearsal and practice opportunities to form new habits and routines
4. Understanding and recognition of when a behavior change is necessary
5. Access to resources that address environmental barriers

The principles of parent support with these indicators of behavior change provide two anchors for this guide. They also provide a rationale by which to understand why the work of parent advisors is critical to effecting positive change for families of children with mental health issues.

Role of Parent Advisors

Parent advisors serve a crucial role in the family support arena. Parents of children with special needs encounter many challenges that make it frustrating and increasingly difficult for them to get their children the help they need. Parent advisors serve as peer support to these parents by providing support and information, facilitating access to appropriate services, being a credible source of information, and modeling effective advocacy and collaborative skills. Parent advisors assist parents while they are "getting up to speed" in learning new skills needed to effectively advocate for their own children. Parent advisors can often function as "trusted intermediaries" in whom parents can confide and candidly share fears and worries, particularly in a highly stigmatized and misunderstood area such as childhood mental illness.

Commonly, parent advisors work with parents in a variety of contexts, including mental health community clinics, schools, hospitals, day treatment programs, and parent-run organizations. Because of the wide variety of systems in which they work as well as the complex issues they must handle, it is often necessary for parent advisors to seek additional training, support, and supervision to assist them in the difficult task of helping families in need.

How to Use This Guide

This guide serves the dual purpose of providing information for those simply looking to improve their professional ability on their own and for those being trained as parent advisors. For those participating in training, this book may be helpful in providing background material about the knowledge and skills needed to be an effective parent advisor. The topics presented in this guide are typically covered in most training and support programs. These programs typically include activities that provide opportunities to practice the skills outlined. A list of training programs is included in Appendix A. Information on the Parent Empowerment Program (PEP) related to this guide is included separately in Appendix B.

Whether this guide is used in isolation or as part of a training program, it is important to know that it requires active practice on your part. Simply reading the book is not sufficient. Implementing the suggestions and answering the self-study questions in each chapter will help increase your knowledge and ability. In addition, you may photocopy the handouts for your own use (see Appendix C for a list).

James Rodriguez

Belinda Ramos

Serene Olin

Geraldine Burton

Overview and Assessment

This chapter provides a brief overview of the skills and knowledge covered throughout the book. It includes a self-assessment so that you can evaluate your current skill set and knowledge base. This evaluation will help you identify the parts of the book that may be most useful to you. We hope you will take an active approach to reading this book. To assist you in your self-study, the end of each chapter includes questions for review and reflection.

Essential Skills

Being a parent advisor is a valuable but challenging job! As a parent advisor, you will need to develop your skills in the following areas.

Listening

Strong listening skills are key to your work as a parent advisor. Listening helps you identify parents' needs. It also helps you build a solid relationship with parents.

Engagement

Engaging parents is the foundation of your work as a parent advisor. Successful engagement allows you to form a trusting relationship with parents. They will then be willing to partner effectively with you to get what they need.

Collaboration

As a parent advisor, you will need to team up with many different people—parents, service providers, teachers, and others. Developing your collaboration skills will help you effectively partner with these individuals.

Boundary Setting

Through your job, you will develop close relationships with the parents you assist. It is important to learn how to set appropriate boundaries around these relationships. For example, you must know when and how to share personal information with parents. You will need to build healthy relationships with parents while taking care of yourself in the process.

Priority Setting

Assisting parents in setting priorities is a valuable undertaking that requires a great deal of skill. Parents often come in with many concerns that can be quite overwhelming. Your priority-setting skills can help parents pave the way in addressing their needs. In addition, helping parents organize and manage their child's records and information is an important task in setting priorities.

Group Management Skills

Parent advisors are often given the task of running parent groups or meetings. Working with parents in a group setting can be a challenging enterprise. Learning the components for facilitating groups and meetings is essential to managing them effectively.

Essential Knowledge

Developing your skills is crucial, but it is also important to increase your knowledge of key information. This will enhance your ability to assist parents in getting their needs met. As a parent advisor, you will need to have working knowledge in the following areas.

Mental Health Evaluation and Diagnosis

Proper assessment is crucial to accessing appropriate care. It can be part of a parent advisor's job to assist families in seeking proper evaluation. You should be able to help parents identify and understand the diagnostic process for psychiatric disorders.

Mental Health System of Care

Helping parents navigate the various systems of care is one of the central tasks of a parent advisor. You should be familiar with types of treatment and service delivery options. You can also prepare parents to get the most out of treatment services.

Childhood Mental Health Disorders

It is important to have a working knowledge of childhood psychiatric disorders and their treatments. As a parent advisor, you may address basic concerns from parents. You can help parents communicate more knowledgeably with mental health professionals and service providers.

The School System and Special Education Options

Parent advisors typically help parents access special education services through the school system. You should be able to help parents understand the role of the school in supporting their child's education. You need to be familiar with the many kinds of services and the different options families have for accessing special education.

Education Laws and Processes

Parent advisors help families understand their children's legal rights and entitlements for a free and appropriate education. You need to know the federal laws that affect a child's education in all the states. You may help guide parents through the process of creating a formal plan to access services.

Assessment of Skills

Before proceeding with this guide, it is important for you to first assess your comfort and ability with essential skills and knowledge. You can then better target areas for improvement in your own professional development. The following self-assessment will help you evaluate your strengths and limitations in key areas for parent advisors. Each section of this assessment corresponds to topics in this book.

Directions: For the following key areas, rate your satisfaction with your own ability. It is important that you rate these as honestly as possible. In addition, think of these statements in terms of the degree by which you *desire* to improve.

Indicate on a scale from 0 to 4 the extent to which each statement describes how satisfied you feel with your abilities. For example, if you somewhat agree with the statement, you would give yourself 2 points. For each skill set, tally all the points of your responses to calculate your total score.

Scale

0	1	2	3	4
Not satisfied at all	Not that satisfied	Somewhat satisfied	Quite satisfied	Highly satisfied
I lack skill in this area.	*I need improvement.*	*There is room for improvement.*	*I need little improvement.*	*I need no improvement.*

Listening, Engagement, Collaboration, and Boundary Setting Skills

In this section, we will ask how satisfied you feel with your ability to engage parents in a supportive working relationship, practice good listening skills, and collaborate with others. You will also rate how able you are to set clear boundaries in your relationship with parents.

Statement   *Points*

1. I have good listening skills (e.g., pick up on nonverbal communication, make empathetic statements, avoid premature problem solving). I am successful in making parents feel at ease in sharing their personal stories with me.   _____

2. I am clearly aware of my own assumptions, attitudes, beliefs, and biases that might influence my work with parents.   _____

3. I am successful at suspending judgment. I do not let my own fears, discomforts, or biases interfere with my ability to understand different kinds of parents.   _____

4. I am effective in addressing parents' beliefs, attitudes, and past experiences that may interfere with their expectations or willingness to seek help.   _____

5. I set boundaries in my work with parents so that I do not get overwhelmed by their problems.   _____

6. I am able to develop good partnerships based on mutual trust and respect for one another's roles and responsibilities.   _____

   Total   _____

Priority-Setting Skills

At first, it can be difficult to identify parents' needs and develop an action plan, particularly when parents have multiple issues they have to confront. Helping parents clarify their problems and set some clear priorities in the work you will do with them is critical.

Statement	Points
1. I know how and what to ask parents in order to clarify their problems or concerns.	_____
2. I am effective at partnering with parents to prioritize their needs.	_____
3. I can effectively partner with parents to develop a realistic plan to address their needs, with clearly specified action steps.	_____
4. I am effective at identifying and problem solving around concrete barriers (e.g., transportation, child care, time, and insurance) that parents may face in seeking help for their children.	_____
5. I am effective at identifying and addressing psychological barriers (e.g., attitudes, beliefs, and past experiences) that may interfere with parents' ability to follow through.	_____
6. I am good at helping parents stay organized in managing their child's case.	_____
Total	_____

Group Management Skills

As a parent advisor, you may find it necessary and useful to run a support group for parents as well as other kinds of groups. Running groups requires skill and experience. If you have little or no experience in facilitating a group or meeting, rate yourself according to the ability you believe you possess.

Statement	Points
1. I know how to prepare for an effective parent group meeting.	_____
2. I can facilitate a group so that all members of a group have an equal chance to participate.	_____

3. I use strategies to keep members of a group from dominating the discussion. _____

4. I am effective at refocusing group members when discussions drift away from a topic. _____

5. I know how to encourage the group to problem solve and think critically when difficulties arise. _____

6. I can maintain a safe environment and constructively manage disagreements and conflicts in a group. _____

Total _____

Mental Health Evaluation, Diagnosis, and Disorders

As a parent advisor, you will have to know about the different types of mental health assessments that are conducted with children. You may help parents understand the diagnostic process and the purpose of diagnostic labels. You may also help direct parents to sources for more information about their child's disorder.

Statement   *Points*

1. I am familiar with the various professionals who can assess children's mental health. _____

2. I am familiar with clinics and agencies in my area that are able to provide appropriate mental health assessments. _____

3. I can educate parents about how to get a mental health evaluation for their child (e.g., what to expect and how to prepare). _____

4. I understand the basic diagnostic process for psychiatric disorders and can explain it to parents. _____

5. I know about the different types of diagnostic labels and how they are used in various settings. _____

6. I have a good understanding of common childhood mental disorders (including causes, diagnosis, and treatments). I am familiar with resources that can provide families with information and assistance. _____

Total _____

Mental Health System of Care

Parent advisors need to know about the kinds of treatment and the many different service options available. You can help parents become knowledgeable consumers of mental health treatment. You may also assist parents in working effectively with their providers.

Statement   *Points*

1. I am familiar with various interventions available to children and families. _____

2. I understand and know how to communicate the concept of "evidence-based practices" in mental health treatment. _____

3. I know the differences between inpatient and outpatient mental health services as well as residential and nonresidential community supports and can communicate those to parents clearly. _____

4. I am familiar with the various emergency service options and can communicate those to parents clearly. _____

5. I can help parents critically evaluate service treatment options for their child and family. _____

6. I know how to help parents communicate concerns about their child's treatment progress to providers. _____

Total _____

The School System and Special Education Options

As a parent advisor, you will have to be able to prepare parents to work with the school system to ensure that their children get the services they need. There are many school-based services and accommodations available to children with special needs. In addition, there are several options for how a child receives a special education.

Statement   *Points*

1. I understand the various terms associated with special education services (e.g., least restrictive environment, related services, and restricted environment). _____

2. I know how to help families access special education services. _____

3. I am familiar with the services and accommodations available to students in a general education setting. _____

4. I am familiar with the different options for special education outside a general education setting. _____

5. I know how to help parents develop a successful partnership with their child's teacher. _____

6. I am familiar with the resources available in the school systems that I work with. _____

Total _____

Education Laws and Processes

To help parents understand their child's entitlements to special education, you must be familiar with federal legislation and how it is carried out in your state. You should be able to guide parents through the different ways to secure services for their child.

Statement	Points
1. I am familiar with federal education laws and how they are implemented in my state.	_____
2. I know the difference between the Individuals with Disabilities Education Act and Section 504 and can communicate this well to parents.	_____
3. I know what an individual education plan (IEP) is and what should be included in an IEP.	_____
4. I am familiar with the types of accommodations that could be offered to children under Section 504.	_____
5. I am familiar with the processes in my area for creating an IEP and a Section 504 plan.	_____
6. I can provide parents with reliable information about their rights and responsibilities within the education system.	_____
Total	_____

Deciphering Your Scores

It is helpful to consider this assessment as a method for considering whether training would be beneficial and appropriate for you. Once you have completed every section, enter your scores on the lines provided.

Totals

Listening, Engagement, Collaboration, and Boundary-Setting
  Skills   _____
Priority-Setting Skills   _____
Group Management Skills   _____
Mental Health Evaluation, Diagnosis, and Disorders   _____
Mental Health System of Care   _____
The School System and Special Education Options   _____
Education Laws and Processes   _____

Score Key:

0–5   Demonstrates great need for development in the specified area. If you feel you have little to no skill in an area, it is important to consider receiving additional support and training if you find the subject critical to your work setting. Reading this guide may be helpful, but you may need further training to meet your needs.

6–11   Demonstrates a desire for significant improvement in the specified area. While you may have some experience or understanding, you may feel that your competence in the given area is below where you expect it to be. While this guide offers the information you may need to improve your skills, additional support and training should be considered, as this will make more of an impact on your abilities.

12–17   Demonstrates an interest and need for minor improvement in the specified area. This guide may help you take your skills and knowledge further by providing formalized strategies and tips for furthering your development.

18–24   Demonstrates little to no need for improvement and comfort within the specified area. More advanced training in the given area may help broaden your expertise.

Making an Action Plan

Once you have completed the assessment section and reviewed your scores, you should bear in mind which areas in need of improvement are priorities for you. There may be an area where you demonstrate a great need for improvement, but the area may hold little importance in your work setting. For example, you may have a low score for Group Management skills, but your work setting may not require this activity of you. On the other hand, there may be areas of high priority where you find yourself in need of moderate to significant improvement. If this is the case, you should consider an action plan for furthering your abilities. While this guide can provide useful and practical information for your professional development, there are also other ways that you can fulfill your action plan:

1. Addressing your needs with your supervisor is always a good place to start. Supervisors are in a position to offer you additional support and consultation. They can also make recommendations for professional advancement.

2. Establishing a peer support group with other parent support workers in your region is an excellent option. This is particularly true for parent advisors who are the sole advisor in their agency. Creating a network of peer support can be highly beneficial in providing a venue for sharing expertise, an opportunity for mentorship, and a foundation for building camaraderie. These groups can meet in person, through conference calls, or by setting up a listserv through the Internet.

3. Taking courses at a local college or university is another good option. You may often be able to receive college credits and credentialing. Many local community colleges offer summer and evening professional certificate courses that can be of interest in your work.

4. Reading relevant books and materials can also be beneficial. Many offer in-depth expertise in the various areas related to families and children with special needs.

5. Receiving training or attending workshops offered by local parent support agencies can be a valuable use of time. The family support field often offers conferences and workshops for those interested in expanding their knowledge base. (See Appendix A for more information.) Attending conferences allows you to network with other advisors and gain knowledge in topics of interest. By inviting the very families you work with to also attend, you can have the opportunity to share the experience with them.

6. Attending a training program offers you the ability to immerse yourself in the topics covered in this guide while receiving ongoing peer support and trainer supervision. A training program such as PEP can be helpful, as it addresses the variety of activities exclusive to parent advisors. (See Appendix A for a list of training programs and Appendix B for more information on PEP.)

Self-Study

After reviewing this chapter, ask yourself the following questions:

1. What essential skills do I need to improve upon? Which ones are priorities for me in my work as a parent advisor?

2. What areas of knowledge do I need to learn more about? Which ones are priorities for me in my work as a parent advisor?

3. What is my action plan for professional development?

Part 1

Building a Strong Foundation
for Working With Parents

Listening, Engagement, and Collaboration Skills

Lisa Hunter Romanelli

Belinda Ramos

Geraldine Burton

Parents and Help Seeking

According to the 1999 Surgeon General report, research has shown that when parents are actively engaged in their children's mental health service planning and treatment, their children have better outcomes (U.S. Department of Health and Human Services, 1999). Yet, for a variety of reasons, parents may be reluctant to be involved in their children's mental health care. Or they may be somehow prevented from being active, informed participants. Even in this enlightened age, mental illness still carries a stigma. Parents often feel blamed (sometimes by care providers themselves) or at fault for their children's emotional and behavioral difficulties. Parents' help-seeking attitudes can be influenced by social and cultural beliefs and their own perceptions and beliefs about mental illness. In addition, their expectations about the benefits of mental health services may affect their willingness to seek help.

Parents come in with varying experiences in their interactions with helping professionals and agencies. These experiences can often leave a significant impact on their beliefs, attitudes, and expectations of other helping professionals and agencies. Negative experiences with the mental health care system or other helping professionals often leave parents apprehensive or distrustful of those claiming to help. Challenges at the system level, including limited services, long wait lists, insurance barriers, and poor-quality care, may further discourage parents from seeking help.

Parents enter the help-seeking process in a variety of ways. They can also have varying comfort levels in getting help. Depending on where parents are at in the help-seeking process, they may have very different needs. For instance, parents may need your help in linking them up to specific services and may not expect more than perhaps a referral. Yet another parent may be overwhelmed with personal challenges, frustrated by the lack of success in navigating various helping institutions, and held up by mixed feelings about getting help. This parent may need more intensive engagement strategies from you over an extended time period.

Essential Ingredients for Engaging Parents

Regardless of where a parent is at in the help-seeking process, engagement is an essential step to building a supportive relationship between you and the parents you work with as a parent advisor. Once engaged and involved, parents will feel more comfortable sharing their concerns with you and working with you in coming up with goals. Engaging a parent can be an ongoing process. There is no cookie-cutter method for what it takes to engage a parent; some parents appreciate and need a little more of one skill over another. However, you can use certain tactics to facilitate this process of engaging parents in their child's well-being. A highly skilled professional has a keen understanding of how to adapt the skills outlined in this chapter to each case. You will need to learn to meet parents where they are at in the process. You must also learn how to work effectively with the various personality styles and individual needs you encounter.

The LEAP Approach

Engagement involves listening, empathizing, agreeing, and partnering with parents. These four steps form the acronym LEAP. A description of each skill follows (adapted from Amador & Johanson, 2000).

Listening

Active listening is the first step in the process of engaging parents. As a parent advisor, you need exceptional listening skills. Listening not only ensures that you understand parents but also demonstrates that you care about what parents are saying. Some of the goals of listening are to get the family's story, to allow parents to vent about their worries and frustrations, and to create a venue for gaining insight into the parents' situation. To facilitate your ability to listen, here are some ways to structure your interactions:

Set aside the time:

In your work, you may have various responsibilities demanding your time and attention. When meeting with parents, however, particularly for the first time, it is vital to provide some structure. This helps ensure that parents feel that their story and needs are important.

Make a formal appointment with the parent:

- Find a time that works well for both of you.
- Address and problem solve around concrete barriers (e.g., transportation and child care) to ensure that the parent is able to make the appointment.

Agree on an agenda:

- Ask parents what they would like to talk about.
- Add anything that you feel is necessary to go over.
- After an agenda is agreed on, give room for parents to express their concerns.

Write it down:

Keeping a record of your conversations with parents will help organize what you have learned. This will also allow you to easily reference the information in the future. However, note taking, particularly in your first meeting, can often be intimidating to parents. It can also make you seem detached from the interaction. Furthermore, slowing parents down in order to collect information from them in the first moments of your interaction can discourage the start of a supportive relationship. Here are some suggestions that can assist you in note taking:

- Allow the first moments of your interaction to be a genuine give-and-take without the distraction of paperwork and writing. You can later take an opportunity to go back and ask parents vital information as you begin to prioritize their needs.
- Ask parents whether they mind your taking some notes during your conversation.
- If parents express discomfort, explain the purpose of the notes and offer to show them what you write.
- If they are still uncomfortable with you writing notes, respect the parents' wishes. Just be sure to write down important facts after the meeting.

Components of Active Listening

Once you have created a comfortable structure for listening, the crucial challenge is to listen actively. Good listening involves more than allowing someone else to talk while keeping silent. Active listening is the process of taking in everything a parent is communicating while conveying genuine interest and concern. Key components of active listening include the following points:

Observe nonverbal gestures (e.g., facial expression and body language). Paying attention to a parent's nonverbal gestures can be an important clue to how the parent feels about a situation.

Encourage expression with empathetic statements and open-ended questions. Sharing concerns about a child's emotional and behavior difficulties can be intimidating, stressful, or overwhelming for a parent. Some parents may be shy, unexpressive, or guarded. Others may believe that you are interested only in the facts rather than what they are really going through. How you approach parents can make a difference in the quality of information you get from parents.

Identify feelings, not just words or behavior (see empathy skills on page 27).

Reflect what you've heard. Repeating back what you heard will serve two purposes: it demonstrates your careful listening and clarifies your interpretation of what has been said. This process lets parents know that you care about their story:

1. When it's your turn to talk, simply repeat back what was said in your own words.
2. Ask "Did I get it right?" or similar questions that indicate your desire to understand.
3. If corrected, repeat back what you heard incorporating the correction and ask again.

Suspend your judgment. It is important to set up a safe and neutral environment so that parents will feel comfortable sharing personal details about their lives. Any judgments or reactions made before hearing the full story may hinder this environment. Not waiting for more information can also lead to incorrect assumptions.

Avoid premature problem solving. In their eagerness to be helpful, it is not uncommon for parent advisors to jump into problem solving prematurely. While early problem solving may resolve some immediate conflicts initially, it does little in establishing an ongoing supportive relationship with parents. It is important to understand that parents not only need concrete services and information but also need to be heard. Active listening is your first step in giving parents a voice in addressing their children's needs.

Good listening can help parents by allowing them to talk and process their experiences. This in itself often reduces tension and anxiety and provides

Tips for Suspending Judgment

People differ in many ways, and in your work as a parent advisor, you will encounter people from various cultures, lifestyles, and backgrounds. Without appreciating and respecting these differences, it is easy to prejudge or stereotype individuals. Setting aside judgments is crucial in successfully keeping our fears, discomforts, or biases from influencing how we interact with others. Follow these tips:

1. Avoid making up your mind before you hear the full story.
2. Be sensitive to cultural differences, beliefs, and customs.
3. Ask questions to clarify why a parent made or makes certain decisions.
4. Avoid assumptions. Listen to the full story before making any statements.
5. Ask yourself how you might account for the parent's behavior and why the parent is responding to the situation in this way.
6. Identify your initial judgments and explore alternative views about the parent and his or her behavior.
7. Accept the parent's story in a positive manner. This is not the same as agreeing with his or her actions.

a sense of relief. It makes the parent feel valued and may contribute significantly to a parent's sense of optimism. Good listening also helps you identify the family's most pressing issues. It allows you to help parents clarify their needs and identify an appropriate course of action.

Empathizing

To empathize with someone is to intellectually or emotionally connect with that person's situations, feelings, and motives. In other words, empathy uses your imagination by placing you in the shoes of another in an attempt to understand that person's experience. It is fairly easy to empathize with someone when you have gone through a similar experience. It is probable that most of us have experienced losing our keys, failing a test, or the death of a loved one. Our memory of the experience helps us recall the feelings of frustration, dismay, or grief associated with these events. The skill in empathizing often comes into play when we need to empathize with events unlike our own experiences. This skill depends on our ability to listen carefully and imagine what it would be like to have gone through the situation. It also involves setting aside quick assumptions and judgments of the person's behavior.

While you may be a parent and, furthermore, a parent of a child with special needs, remember that reactions to similar situations can vary greatly. One parent finding out that his or her child has a serious illness may react with relief about identifying the cause of the child's difficulties. Another parent may be angry or have difficulty coming to terms with the illness. Empathy requires you to allow parents to tell you the how and why of their thoughts, feelings, and behavior. In turn, being empathetic gives you greater ability to be compassionate, interested, and supportive in your role.

It is important to know and understand that parents of children with special needs often experience stressors above and beyond parents of typically developing children. Issues may include parenting difficulties, stigma, and barriers to obtaining services. These parents often experience blame for the conditions they are under from family members and professionals alike. This blame is a result of a lack of sympathetic understanding for the stressors and strains experienced by raising a child with mental health problems. Your role is crucial in providing a space where parents can begin to vent their concerns and frustration and feel accepted, recognized, and valued for their efforts.

Active listening is central to empathizing. The more you are attuned to what a parent communicates, the easier it is to imagine how it must feel to be in his or her place. As you listen, it is important to verbally express your empathy to the parent. The following empathetic statements can help validate parents' experiences, frustrations, and fears. They can also help increase their sense of being effective parents.

- "If that happened to me, I would feel the same way."
- "I imagine that was really frustrating."
- "I can only imagine how hard that must have been."
- "You've gone through a lot to help your child."
- "It sounds like you really love your child."

It is important to note that empathizing is not necessarily agreeing with a parent's actions and attitudes. Rather, you are attempting to look at the situation from the parent's perspective. You may disagree with a parent's beliefs or actions, but your ability to demonstrate acceptance and understanding is an essential part of forming a working relationship with a parent. Such empathy can be critical in encouraging parents to share their concerns and needs more openly.

Encouraging Expression Through Empathetic, Open-Ended Questions

Typically, open-ended questions can help create more of a dialogue between you and the parent. Closed-ended questions tend to lead to short responses, like "yes" and "no," that provide very little information or insight on how you can help. An example of a closed-ended question would be "How often do you talk with your child's teacher?" This question more than likely would lead to a short, factual answer. On the other hand, an open-ended way of getting at this same information would be "How would you describe your relationship with your child's teacher?" Following up with other open-ended questions encourages a parent to express the full story.

Here are some examples of statements and questions that help set the stage for an empathetic dialogue. These kinds of questions are important to remember when you are trying to learn more about parents, help them to talk through their feelings, and encourage a supportive relationship with you.

- "I want to better understand what you went through. Can you tell me what the experience was like for you?"
- "I imagine you felt angered. What are some of your beliefs about the situation?"
- "That must have been very frustrating for you. What helped you get through it?"
- "You did the best you could given the situation. What are some of the things you are confident you did right?"

Agreeing

Listening and empathizing with a parent helps set a foundation for a collaborative working relationship. Getting a parent's full story is important in the beginning, as it allows a parent advisor to clarify a parent's most pressing needs and concerns. While parents may need an outlet to vent their concerns, they also need someone to help them more clearly think through the steps they should take in addressing their needs. Once you have reached an understanding of the parents' perspective and needs, you can work together to identify and agree on an appropriate plan of action.

Even when parents may not have a sense of what to do next, they can often express what they would like to see happen as a result. Here are some sample statements and questions that you could use to help the parents you work with identify an acceptable action plan.

- "There are a lot of ways that this could possibly be addressed, but I am interested in knowing what you would like to see happen."
- "What would you like to see change in the next month?"
- "Your family is very important to you, and I want to be sure that whatever is working right now is incorporated into our plan of action. Are you able to tell me what is working for your family?"

In developing a plan, it is essential to allow parents to consider what is important to them. This should be a guiding practice in supporting families. Remember that you may not always agree with a parent on a specific course of action. Your role as a parent advisor is to provide families with accurate information so that they can begin to consider options that suit their needs. If you are concerned about a parent's choice of action, you might consider helping a parent assess how achievable the plan may be. For example, you may ask, "How has this worked for you in the past?" Or you may provide information to correct misconceptions parents may have about how their plan will work. You may then help parents consider alternative courses of action. While providing answers and solutions to families' problems may seem like the quickest way of resolving matters, it does little in terms of empowering parents. A key role of parent advisors is to help parents actively think through their choices and consider alternative options. The priority skills chapter of this guide outlines steps you could take to help parents clarify and prioritize their concerns and put an action plan into effect.

Partnering

The last step of the LEAP approach involves solidifying a strong partnership with parents in order to achieve the agreed-on goals. This process already began during the first three steps (listening, empathizing, and agreeing). During the partnering step, it is important to identify specifically what you will do and what the parent will do to achieve the agreed-on goals. Establishing a working relationship involves a mutual understanding that solutions should come through your partnership. The goal of the partnership is to help the parent become an active agent of change on behalf of his or her family.

Strong partnerships are based on trust and mutual respect for one another's roles and responsibilities. As a parent advisor, it is important to clarify your role in order to set clear and realistic expectations, develop trust, and avoid disappointments. At the same time, it is wise not to make assumptions about a parent's role and responsibilities. The parents that you work with may differ in their ability and degree to which they may need hand holding. Having an honest conversation with parents can be a good place to start in establishing an alliance. Be clear with one another as to what your roles are, how you can help one another, and what you can and cannot do. This communication is vital to forming trust in the partnership.

In partnering with parents on a plan of action, you should establish your roles in this plan from the outset. Be up front about any potential constraints. For example, some clinic-based parent advisors work with parents for a specified period of time. In that case, a discussion on the time frame for services and a plan for how a parent should proceed from that point would be in order. This could help both parties develop more realistic expectations and avoid disappointments.

At the same time, it is essential to communicate with parents your desire and willingness to do your best in your work with them. They should be made to feel that your relationship with them is based on a trusting partnership. They should feel comfortable questioning and sharing doubts or disagreements about the plan of action. Such a partnership can serve as an important model by reinforcing their abilities. Through your work together, parents will become more confident in securing services for their family and asserting their wishes when matters are not working in their favor.

In short, the following basic steps can help solidify a partnership:

1. Clarify your role and responsibilities to the parents. You may want to ask parents to express their understanding of what they should expect from you.
2. Address any areas where the expectations are beyond your scope or capability.
3. Put any plan of action into writing. Clearly outline needs or objectives, how and when these will be addressed, who will be responsible, and the desired outcome.
4. Assure parents that plans can always be revisited if they feel uncomfortable or dissatisfied with how things are progressing.

Three Essential "R's" for Engagement

In addition to LEAP, it is also important to remember three essential "R's" when engaging parents. These additional tips provide target areas that have been recognized to help build a working alliance with parents. The three essential "R's" are:

- Real conversations about real issues
- Reducing stigma
- Recognizing barriers

Real Conversations About Real Issues

Speak honestly with parents about their concerns, their needs, your mutual responsibilities, and future plans. Strongly consider the interests of the family and what they are most concerned with. Although parents may be concerned about their child's mental health needs, they may have other pressing needs and concerns. These may get in the way of parents' ability to effectively address their child's mental health issues. Parent advisors must be willing to help parents identify how these concerns may interfere with their efforts or even worsen a child's mental health problems. Parent advisors then must be ready to work with parents to problem solve around these concerns. Addressing these "extra" concerns through conversation and problem solving can be very productive. It can greatly increase parents' ability and motivation to address their concerns in relation to their child's mental health problems. Some characteristics of real conversations are the following:

- A focus on immediate concerns of the family
- Giving help to the family in negotiating with other agencies that may be involved, such as the school and child welfare systems
- Helping the family gain access to other social services or resources (e.g., Medicaid, Supplemental Security Income, and Temporary Assistance for Needy Families)

Reducing Stigma

Mental health can still be a touchy subject in our culture. In addition, there is a lot of false information being circulated. As such, it is not uncommon for parents to feel embarrassment or shame about their child's diagnosis or treatment. It is important to help parents decrease or eliminate these feelings. This will put parents in a better position to partner with you and assist their child in obtaining services. When discussing stigma, remember that it may be a sensitive issue (e.g., if parents have just learned about the diagnosis, it might be difficult for them to accept). Some steps for reducing stigma are the following:

1. Raise the issue. For example, it is a common misconception that children's mental health problems are simply misbehavior resulting from bad

parenting. Hearing this said or implied by friends, family, and/or doctors could have a severe effect on a parent's self-esteem.

2. Provide information to demonstrate that this belief is not true.
3. Allow parents to express their beliefs and attitudes about mental disorders and reasons why they feel uncomfortable. This step is very important.
4. Consider referring parents to a support group to help normalize their feelings and experiences.
5. Work with parents to figure out ways to deal with people in their lives who promote their feelings of stigma.
6. Address the issue of stigma when families are out in public (e.g., on public transportation or in restaurants).

Recognizing Barriers

Addressing barriers is crucial to achieving success in meeting goals. These barriers need to be attended to in a flexible manner. Overlooking obstacles or dealing with them in a rigid way decreases parents' sense that they can get what their family needs. Work with parents to identify and resolve possible obstacles to seeking help for their child. Potential obstacles to seeking services include the following:

- Transportation problems
- Previous negative experiences with the mental health system
- Resistance from family members
- Language barriers
- Scheduling conflicts
- Lack of child care
- Insurance barriers
- Lack of knowledge about how to navigate the system

Putting Engagement Skills to Work

It is important to remember that the engagement strategies described in this chapter are highly interrelated and are not intended to be used in isolation. Depending on the parent you are working with, you will pull from these skills in various ways. When engaging parents and building meaningful relationships with them, the most important thing to understand is that the key skills are tools for keeping a family's best interest in mind.

Self-Study

After reviewing this chapter, ask yourself the following questions:

1. What are some things that affect parents' help-seeking attitudes?

2. What are some steps I can take to improve my listening skills?

3. How can I overcome the impulse to judge a parent when I disagree with how the parent is dealing with his or her child?

4. What roles and responsibilities do I feel comfortable with in my partnership with parents?

5. What is the biggest challenge I have encountered when trying to engage parents in the past? What can I do to improve my strategy on this issue?

James Rodriguez

Belinda Ramos

Lisa Hunter Romanelli

Geraldine Burton

Boundary-Setting Skills

Privacy and Confidentiality

Parents share extremely sensitive and personal information with parent advisors. In order to develop a trusting and strong working relationship with parents, it is critical to discuss privacy and confidentiality with them. Parents need to know what information can be kept completely confidential and the limits of confidentiality. Information that indicates that someone is in danger of harm to him- or herself or others must be reported—in some cases to the proper authorities. The limits to confidentiality are clear when abuse is suspected or occurring or when someone is threatening or being threatened with physical harm.

Some instances are less clear about whether information indicates imminent harm or requires a report. For instance, a parent may disclose a history of domestic violence or knowledge that his or her teenager is using drugs. This information would be critical to anyone working with the child or family, but the parent may not be ready for others to know. In such instances, it is important to discuss the issue with the parent before you share it with others.

Confidentiality is also limited if someone else is present when information is shared. This is why it is important to have conversations in which sensitive or personal information might be shared in private settings. Confidential information, obviously, can be shared with others at the parents' request.

It is critical to discuss these limits to confidentiality with parents at the very beginning of your working relationship. Trust in the relationship will be weakened if parents are not informed that certain information needs to be shared with others or if private information is shared without their knowledge.

Balancing Professional and Personal Needs

Parent advisors are often driven by their passion and compassion when working with families in need. They will often go the extra mile in order to engage and assist families in the help-seeking process. However, like other helping professionals, you should always take the time to consider how to balance your professional demands and personal needs. The desire to help others can often keep parent advisors from attending to personal needs. You may find that you repeatedly dismiss personal needs because of professional demands. This pattern can put you at risk for burnout and stress-related health concerns. The outcome can greatly diminish your ability to help others or to function effectively in your personal life.

As a parent advisor, it can be difficult to take care of yourself while trying to help others. It is important to be aware of your own needs and struggles when working with other families. If you become too overwhelmed with other people's problems, you may not be able to take care of your own responsibilities. Likewise, if you share too many of your own current struggles with families, they may not trust your ability to do your job, or they may feel weighted down by your personal concerns.

Support Exercise

Take this opportunity to consider the following important reflective questions. You may want to jot your answers down in a notebook.

- Whom can you turn to for help with your personal and professional responsibilities?
- Who are the people that you can share your own concerns with?
- What is your plan for keeping your personal problems out of your work?

In addition, take a moment to make a list of resources (e.g., close friends, support groups, family, or special activities) to access when feeling overwhelmed or in need of additional support. This is also a good exercise to recommend to parents.

Tips for Keeping Healthy

Here are some useful tips for keeping yourself healthy:

Addressing Your Own Needs

- Discuss personal problems with friends and family (not parents you work with).
- Access a supervisor or knowledgeable peer to provide support on issues with parents.
- Seek help from another parent advisor or agency when you're overloaded with cases or in need of additional input or support.
- If you are feeling overwhelmed, take time in your day to think about your own needs. Then follow through with whatever you may have decided is necessary.

Taking Care of Yourself

- Eat a healthy diet. Getting plenty of fruits, vegetables, and water provides your body with the nutrition it needs for thinking and moving.
- Exercise regularly. This will help your physical and mental health. Going for a walk is a great way to relax!
- Take time to wind down by involving yourself in activities that help you de-stress. This can even happen in small pockets of time. Use your favorite pastimes or hobbies as a starting point.
- Make sure you are getting enough rest and sleep. Getting the appropriate amount of rest is one the biggest factors in keeping yourself physically, mentally, and emotionally healthy.
- Make good use of your vacation time. When it is time to relax and take a break, stick to it. Whether you stay in town or go away, use this time to fuel your own life.
- Read or watch something that inspires you. Books, documentaries, movies, plays, and so on can all provide material that may be a great source of encouragement for you.
- Keep a journal. Writing down your thoughts and feelings or documenting your journey can be therapeutic. It also allows you the opportunity to go back and trace your personal growth.
- Know your own limitations. Knowing when you are "doing too much" or "going too far" should be something that you are able to determine and willing to address.

Sharing Personal Information

At times you may want to share personal information with parents to build rapport. Your own story may be the very reason why you decided to become a parent advisor. It may help provide encouragement to another parent. Sharing personal information can do the following:

- Normalize others' concerns
- Encourage a positive relationship by conveying understanding of others' experiences
- Describe new ways of viewing a situation and possible options
- Provide hope by modeling success in effectively managing the challenges of raising a child with mental health needs

However, when sharing personal information, you should be careful to use your judgment. Sharing personal information inappropriately can cloud the relationship and diminish your credibility. Sharing personal information is unhealthy if it does the following:

- Takes up valuable time in a non-goal-directed way
- Is done in a "can you top this" fashion (e.g., "You think you have problems? Let me tell you about mine.")
- Done in an advice-giving fashion
- Is made in an attempt to seek approval
- Is done for your benefit and not for that of the client

Maintaining a Healthy Working Relationship

Another aspect of good professional practice is to set boundaries for your working relationship with parents. The work of a parent advisor is one that involves flexibility and availability. Some work environments require you to accomplish tasks with parents within a 9–5 time frame. However, needs from parents can arrive at any time and can push the limits of what is reasonable for you. Striking a balance between your responsibilities, your desire to help, and how much of your time you are willing to give is a personal decision-making process. Your consideration should include what you need to keep yourself healthy, what is beneficial for the parents you work with, and the rules and regulations your agency has in place.

Here are some tips for keeping the working relationship healthy:

- Decide how and when you will be available to the families with whom you work. Some parent advisors are available whenever needed, while others may choose to set certain times for availability. Whatever you decide, make sure to let families know how and when they can reach you.

- Consistency is essential in a trusting relationship. However you schedule your time, make sure that you are reliably available to parents.
- Know your agency's policy on interacting with parents outside of work-related functions. Parents may invite you to special family functions; however, some agencies may not allow this. In this case, be up front about such matters in order to avoid any confusion in the relationship.

Empowering Parents

Setting boundaries in your work also comes into play in negotiating your role with parents. You may need to decide how much hand holding is appropriate with a parent. Or you may need to decide what to do when the working relationship becomes burdensome. Your role involves supporting parents in addressing their needs. The demands on you can be great when parents have limited ability to effectively take direct control in advocating for their child or family.

Your goal as a parent advisor is to supportively equip parents with the knowledge and skill necessary to effectively advocate for themselves. This process of empowerment should begin at the outset of your relationship. You should continually build opportunities for parents to develop an increasing confidence in their ability to advocate for themselves. Some ways of encouraging this include the following:

1. Let parents take control and initiative in activities from the outset of your work with them. This expectation can be communicated as you clarify your roles and responsibilities to one another.
2. Revisit your mutual responsibilities for every new activity or goal in your work with a parent.
3. Model skills for parents when necessary. Role plays can be a helpful tool in demonstrating how to apply various skills or knowledge.
4. Provide opportunities for parents to practice skills in real situations. For example, if you are working with parents on being more assertive, allow them to try these skills out on a phone call or in meeting with service providers.
5. Provide encouragement and constructive feedback on skills parents try out. Follow up with them after attempts to apply a skill or knowledge in a real situation.
6. Discuss obstacles when parents are afraid or unsure or do not follow through on their part in a plan. Spend time trying to understand underlying attitudes or beliefs that might be holding parents back and problem solve around them.

Self-Study

After reviewing this chapter, ask yourself the following questions:

1. Do I understand the limits to privacy and confidentiality in my work with parents?

2. What aspect of boundary setting do I struggle with most?

3. What are some things I can do to relax and get my mind off work?

4. What are some healthy limits I can set to better my work life?

5. What am I comfortable doing for a parent? What am I not comfortable with?

6. What should I do if a parent wants to be too close? What is my definition of too close?

James Rodriguez

Adam Stein

Lisa Hunter Romanelli

Priority-Setting Skills

The previous chapters discussed ways to establish a strong working relationship with parents using engagement, listening, collaboration, and boundary-setting skills. When you first meet parents, the most important thing you can do is to listen actively to their story. Once you have offered a supportive ear, you can ask specific questions to clarify your understanding of the parents' concerns. Then you can begin to try to set priorities about actions that need to be taken on behalf of parents' children.

In your work as a parent advisor, you are likely to encounter upset parents with many concerns. Indeed, parent advisors are often called on to work with the most distressed parents. In these cases, it may be difficult to identify and prioritize parents' needs and even more difficult to develop a plan to address their needs. These needs can be overwhelming, and you are likely to wonder, "How can I possibly address all the concerns of this family?" Just like a juggler cannot keep all the balls in the air at the same time, you as a parent advisor cannot address a family's multiple needs simultaneously. Rather, you must prioritize a family's needs. Remember that it is important to include parents in the priority-setting process.

This chapter provides some specific strategies to help you clarify and prioritize parents' needs. It outlines how to collect important information about the family. It also discusses how to identify action steps and barriers to addressing needs as well as strategies for overcoming barriers to planned actions.

Clarifying Parents' Needs

Parents will often come in with some very specific concerns about their child. These may include problems in the parent–child relationship and managing their child's behavior at home, at school, or in the community. The first step in setting priorities with parents is clarifying their concerns. It is often important to start here because it demonstrates to parents that you take their most immediate needs seriously. It shows that you have an interest in finding out more about what their pressing needs really are. This is often easier said than done, especially when parents have many concerns or are experiencing one or more crises. The following are some ways that you can use your active listening skills to clarify parents' needs.

Step 1: Identify All Concerns

Allow parents to vent their many concerns. If necessary, reflect back what you've heard and make empathic statements as discussed in Chapter 3. Then ask for other concerns they have about their child or themselves. The following are some examples:

- "So it sounds like you're very frustrated with the school calling you all the time about your child's behavior. Do you have other concerns about your child?"
- "Your relationship with your child is very important to you. Are there other concerns you have about your child?"
- "All these concerns appear to make you (upset, sad, or angry). Are there some other concerns you have about yourself or the rest of your family?"

Step 2: Prioritize Needs

Once you have allowed parents to vent and express their many concerns, you can begin to prioritize their needs. You can either ask parents directly or, again, use your listening skills. The following are some examples of questions you can ask:

- "As we have talked about you and your situation, I've heard that your main concern is _____. What do you think? Is that the most pressing issue for you at this time?"

If parents express many concerns:

- "What are your main concerns or top two concerns?"

Step 3: Assess Specific Needs

Once you have identified the parents' main concern(s), you can then begin to understand the context of these concerns. Here are some questions you can ask parents to help clarify their needs. Keep in mind that if there is more than one concern, you might have to ask the following questions for each stated concern. In this case, you may have to work hard to keep a parent on task with one concern before you move on to others. In order to develop a targeted action plan, it is important that you fully understand the situations or conditions under which problems occur. It is premature to develop a plan before such an assessment is done.

 1. *"Where does the problem occur?"*

Problems generally can occur at home, at school, or in the community. If parents report that the problem occurs at home, it would still be important to ask if the problem occurs in other places.

 2. *"When does the problem occur?"*

Be as specific as possible. If it is something that occurs every day, then ask about the time of day. If the problem occurs once a week, ask what part of the week (weekdays, weekends, and so on). In addition, always ask how often the problem occurs.

 3. *"Who is involved in the problem?"*

This is critically important because the things that often trigger problem behaviors are other people. Find out as much as possible about the people that might be involved in the problem. This will give you ideas about who will need to be involved in making necessary changes.

 4. *"How long has this been a concern, and what has the parent or others tried in the past to address it?"*

This question can provide important information on how chronic or temporary the concern might be and what has been done to address the concern. It also helps identify barriers at the child, family, community, or system level that may make it difficult for parents to successfully address the problem.

Collecting Information

Once you have clarified the parents' needs, it is tempting to jump to making plans and suggesting solutions based on your own experience or your experience with other parents with similar problems. However, once you have listened to the parents' story and asked questions to determine their needs, the next step is to collect additional information. This information will help you better understand parents' concerns and needs in a broader context of their everyday living situation. It will give you a better idea of what the best course of action might be, given the particular circumstances of the family. Following are seven critical areas of information to obtain.

Contact Information

This includes the client's name, phone number, address, work phone, cell phone, e-mail address, and so on. When you obtain contact information, be sure to ask parents how best to contact them and where they should *not* be contacted. In some cases, this may be for practical reasons, such as when parents don't want to be contacted at work because employers frown on it. In other cases, safety may be the critical issue. For example, a mother living in a domestic violence situation may not want the abusive partner to know that she is getting help outside the home.

Referral Source

Obtain the name and contact information of the person who made the referral. If the parent was referred from another agency or individual, you will want to get that information *and* permission to contact. The referral source might be able to provide valuable information that helps you better understand the parents' circumstances.

Family System

Ask for the names and ages of all family/household members. This information will instantly give you a great deal of information. You will immediately know whether a spouse is present, if there are extended family members in the home, and the number of children and their ages. The structure of the family (e.g., nuclear families, extended families, or multifamily homes) can provide a lot of information about what family life might be like for the parent. It can give some clues about the presence of risks or resources that might be available in the immediate family.

Social Support System

Get a description of the social supports available to the parent. Social supports are the people whom individuals turn to when they need help in various areas of their lives. Sometimes people need financial assistance, help with child care, a supportive ear, advice on child rearing or relationships, or simply someone to have fun with. A strong social support system can alleviate many of the stresses that a parent of a child with special needs might face. A weak or nonexistent

Circles of Support

In each circle, fill in the name or names of the people who support you in that way. Draw a line between the "You" and the name of each support person. Use the different kinds of lines (see key below) to assess the relative strength of the relationship.

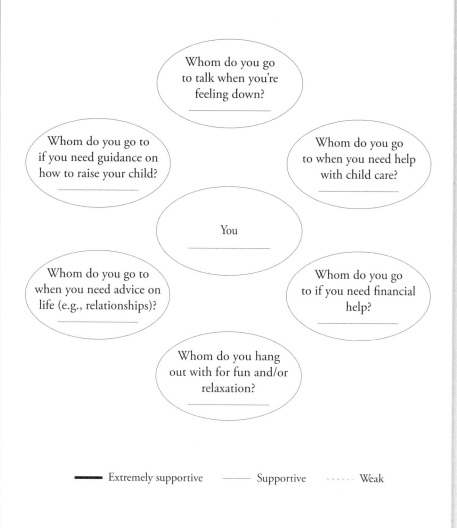

support system places the parent and child at greater risk for poor mental health outcomes.

The Circles of Support worksheet is an example of an easy way to assess a parent's social support system. It can be used to identify the presence or absence of social supports in different areas. It can also be used to indicate the strength of the relationship between the parent and the person providing that area of support.

Community

Get a description of the family's community. The neighborhoods in which families live can greatly impact family and child development. It is important to ask families about the general safety of their neighborhoods (e.g., the presence of gangs, drug use, and illegal activities). Find out about the connection or relationship with neighbors. Identify the location of resources in their neighborhoods (see list of systems in the next section). Determine the general appearance and condition (e.g., type of housing) of the family's home or surrounding homes.

Information on whom the family identifies with socially or culturally may also be useful. It may provide insight on the family's beliefs and attitudes toward mental health and help seeking. It can also give you an idea of the level of support or opposition families may be facing in trying to carry out an action plan.

Contact With Systems

It is important to know what, if any, contact the family has with the following systems:

- Other mental health agencies
- School or the board of education
- Hospitals or clinics
- Legal system
- Child welfare system
- Recreational programs
- Religious/spiritual organizations
- Social service agencies
- Support groups

Keep a few things in mind as you inquire. First, with each system, you want to determine their general satisfaction with services or contacts in that system.

Understanding past experiences with other systems, especially mental health agencies and the school system, will give you insights into parents' attitudes and skepticism about the helpfulness of service providers. This could be an important obstacle to overcome in getting them the services they need.

Second, information on other systems will give you an idea of services that have been tried in the past and failed. More important, it may give you access to parents' perception of why these services may have failed.

Finally, remember to continue to practice care, compassion, and empathy skills as you ask about these systems. Past experiences with these systems or services might draw out some very intense emotions in parents. Some systems (e.g., child welfare) may elicit stronger reactions than others (e.g., recreational programs). Be prepared to listen and respond empathetically when parents express frustration, sadness, or anger when discussing past experiences.

Strengths/Resources

Gather information about the family's strengths. Last but not least, you should ask parents about the personal strengths they have developed over the course of their lives. While sharing information during the collection process, parents may identify certain strengths. For example, they may have a strong

---

Tips for Collecting Information

Most likely, your agency will have a form you can use to record this information. If your agency does not have a form, you can develop one using they key areas listed in this chapter. To successfully gather this information from parents, you will need to continue to use your listening and engagement skills. Here are a few additional tips:

- Be conversational. Do not read directly from the form. Be familiar with the questions that need to be answered beforehand.
- Be sensitive. If a parent becomes emotional during the intake process, set the form aside momentarily to console the parent.
- Meet in a private, quiet place to collect the information.
- Think ahead. If you know parents are going to need certain documents or be asked for information they may not readily know, tell them about information they may need to bring.

family or social support system, or they might be receiving great services. When parents do not mention it themselves, it is important to help them identify personal strengths. Ask parents to share what they think their personal strengths are. In cases where parents have a hard time doing this, reflect back on the qualities you have seen demonstrated as they shared their stories, whether it is persistence, patience, concern, or wisdom.

Developing a Case Management Book

One last note on gathering information: it is important for parents to document the health, education, and mental health care needs of their children. There are three good reasons to keep information organized and available. First, providers may often want to get specific information about a child's school history or previous evaluations in order to make well-informed diagnoses. Second, parents may need to provide documentation of prior services in order to advocate for additional services or more intensive services (e.g., requesting day treatment to replace outpatient care). Third, documentation of a child's treatment history (e.g., behavior plans, medication history, or therapy) can be used to advocate for continuing approaches that worked in the past or avoiding approaches that were not effective.

For all these reasons, we recommend that parents accumulate as much information about their child as possible and organize it in a case management book. This could be a useful exercise for parent advocates to complete with parents. You can help parents collect all the information they have about their child's educational, health, and mental health history. This should include psychiatric of psychological evaluations, school evaluations, individualized education plans (IEPs), report cards, treatment plans, behavior plans, medication history, and letters and other correspondences from schools and providers. The information can be organized in a three-ring binder with separate sections for the type of information (e.g., school, health, and mental health). We also recommend that parents keep a separate section for their own notes about the child where they can record any changes they notice during treatment, side effects to medications, and questions to ask service providers. This case management book should be kept up to date and brought to doctor and school visits.

Identifying Action Steps

At this point in the process, you should have established a strong working relationship through listening and engagement skills, identified one or a couple of key priority needs, and gathered important information. It is now possible to identify action steps that parents can take to effectively manage their children's mental health needs. Action steps can include things like setting up a meeting with the child's teacher, taking the child for a psychological or psychiatric evaluation, requesting a referral for special education services, or talking with the child's doctor about medication.

Action steps are usually best associated with larger goals. For example, in talking with a mother about her child, a priority—and a much broader goal—may be reducing the stress in the mother's life. This kind of broad goal can involve specific action steps like engaging in specific self-care activities, getting respite care, or getting therapy. The priority needs will differ from family to family, but the action steps should always be clear, straightforward, and achievable. They should include what needs to be done (e.g., calling an agency), who will do it and who might assist (e.g., parent advocate will provide mother with resources, and mother will call), and a time frame for accomplishing each step or specific task. See the example of an action plan form.

Identifying Potential Barriers

Even the best-laid plans are likely to fail unless the parent is ready, willing, and able to follow up. It is important to identify potential barriers to successful follow-through on action steps. For example, a parent with a child with mental health care needs may need to be evaluated for special education by the local school district. However, the parent does not know how to request an evaluation, has fears about her child getting labeled, has had negative interactions with school staff, and does not think that special education will help. All these very common obstacles make it very unlikely that the parent will follow up on this specific action step (namely, to request an evaluation).

As you are listening to parents and asking questions to determine their needs, it is important to identify and directly ask parents about barriers that may prevent them from successfully addressing these needs. *Identifying and working through potential barriers is a critical discussion. It can increase parents' willingness or ability to follow through with a course of action. Unfortunately, it is also often overlooked by many professionals working with parents, including advisors, teachers, and clinicians.*

Common Barriers

There are many different reasons why people do not follow through on a plan of action. Barriers to action may be concrete or psychological. In order to understand parents' behavior, it is important to consider factors that might influence their willingness or intention to follow through with the plan. Common concrete barriers that affect parents' willingness to act include time, transportation, child care, and financial cost. Common psychological barriers include thoughts, feelings, expectations of benefit, and attitudes (e.g., stigma). In particular, past experiences with school systems, mental health providers, or other helping agencies have a powerful impact on parents' willingness to engage in a plan. Such experiences need to be explored and parent concerns addressed.

Even when parents are willing and have good intentions of following a plan of action, other barriers may make it difficult for parents to translate their intention into action. For such parents, barriers such as knowledge, skill, and ability might be the reason for lack of follow-through. For example, some parents may need information on medications, their benefits and risks, and alternative treatment options. Or they may need to be coached on the types of questions to ask a provider in order to better assess their options. Without knowing how to access such information, they may not consistently support a treatment for their child. Other parents may need information on the structure of an IEP meeting at a school as well as coaching on assertiveness skills in order to advocate for special services. Other barriers include environmental constraints such as the lack of available services or insurance issues.

Things to Keep in Mind About Barriers

Some barriers are easier to identify than others. Regardless of the type of barrier, it will be unlikely that the parent will follow through on action steps unless it is addressed. Never assume that the parent is ready, willing, and able to follow up on specific action steps just because a need is prioritized and action steps are suggested. Keep the following in mind with regard to barriers:

1. Always assume and anticipate that some barriers exist. In some cases, they might be small and easy to deal with. In other cases, they will be critical and difficult to overcome.
2. Put barriers on the table. You can ask parents directly about barriers to certain actions. Or you can explore them as you are clarifying needs or gathering information.
3. "Roll with resistance." When parents do not follow up on specific action steps, view it as an opportunity to identify and address barriers. We sometimes view inaction or poor follow-through in negative terms: disinterest, laziness, ignorance, or defiance. While parent "resistance" might be frustrating, it is important to explore the reasons for inaction and problem solve around them.

Example of an Action Plan

Parent: ___Mary___ Child: ___Jason___ Parent Advisor: Anita___

Instructions: List each goal/objective in specific detail and identify who will carry out the action step and a deadline for completing the action step.

Goal/Objective: Obtain a psychological evaluation to try to see if Jason's problems at school are behavioral/emotional or a learning challenge.

Action Step	Who will do it?	By when?
1. Provide list of agencies that that perform psychological assessments	Anita	End of day
2. Prepare mother with questions to ask agencies when calling	Anita	End of meeting
3. Contact each agency for appointment/information	Mary	End of week
4. Prepare for agency visit (e.g.,questions to ask)	Mary/Anita	After appointment is made

Goal/Objective: Set up conference with school to discuss Jason's progress with school difficulties.

Action Step	Who will do it?	By when?
1. Call teacher to let her know that request will be made	Mary	Tomorrow
2. Write letter to principal requesting a meeting	Mary/Anita	End of meeting
3. Gather all information related to past history of child's difficulties	Mother/Jason	End of week
4. Follow-up with phone call to school to check receipt of letter	Mary	3 days after letter is sent
5. Prepare for meeting.	Mary/Anita	Before meeting takes place

Addressing Barriers: Problem-Solving Strategies

The final step in setting and addressing priority needs is to problem solve around the barriers to action steps. The following are some strategies that can be used to overcome some of the common barriers mentioned earlier.

Explore Concerns

Parents may not always be fully aware or willing to discuss barriers or challenges. It might be helpful for parent advisors to list some of the common barriers parents experience or encounter. This can help normalize parents' difficulties in following through with an action plan. Being empathetic, keeping an open mind, and suspending judgments can result in a productive discussion. The goal is to help parents feel more supported and obtain what they need in order to move forward with a plan.

Teach New Skills

This is particularly helpful strategy when the barrier to action steps is a lack of skills. A good example of this is when parents need to advocate on their own behalf but do not have good assertive communication skills. Role plays are an excellent way to teach new skills. People often feel uncomfortable doing role plays, but role plays provide important practice opportunities. Constructive feedback from these activities can help better prepare parents in using a new skill or knowledge in an unfamiliar situation.

Provide Information

Much of the material in later chapters of this book provides valuable information that parents can use. You may also have to work with parents on finding necessary information in other locations like the Internet. Resource guides are also often available from organizations (see Appendix A). Often, information can demystify a disorder. It may allow parents to view a problem in a new light (e.g., "I'm not a bad parent") and help motivate positive action.

Highlight Cost and Benefits

Sometimes parents need to explore the cost and benefits of taking an action versus keeping things the same. A simple but effective strategy for helping parents make decisions is to do a cost-benefit analysis. This involves exploring the benefits as well as costs of taking an action versus keeping things the same. Following is an example of a cost-benefit analysis for a parent who has mixed feelings about getting her child evaluated for special education.

Example of Cost-Benefit Analysis

Action: Getting Child Evaluated

Benefits of Taking Action:

1. My child will get an appropriate education.
2. My child will get more services in the school.
3. The school will stop hassling me.
4. My child will do better in school.

Costs of Taking Action:

1. The evaluation will cost money.
2. I will have to take time off from work.
3. I will have to deal with school/district red tape.
4. My family/friends will not approve.

Benefits of Not Taking Action:

1. My child will not get labeled.
2. My child will remain in the same school/class.

Costs of Not Taking Action:

1. School will continue to threaten to report me for educational neglect.
2. I will feel like a bad parent.

This process can be effective if you keep a few things in mind. First, allow the parent to share all her concerns. *Do not comment* (except to encourage the parent to say more) until she has listed all the costs and benefits. You can, however, provide some suggestions if a parent is stuck.

Second, it is very important to continue to use all your active listening skills and, especially, *suspend judgment.* You may not feel that having to take time off from work is a legitimate reason for inaction, but you will have to set that aside for this exercise.

Third, validate all the parent's concerns. Even if you don't agree with them, you can validate the parent for her honesty.

Finally, after you have allowed the parent to share, you can address concerns and misconceptions. For instance, in the previous example, you can answer questions about the costs of evaluations.

This process will be helpful if you view it as a strategy for exploring parents' concerns and ambivalence about a particular action. Try to avoid seeing it as a way of convincing parents of doing something they are not ready to do. Allow the parents to come to their own conclusions.

Self-Study

After reviewing this chapter, ask yourself the following questions:

1. What are some common questions I can ask parents to help determine and prioritize their needs?

2. When collecting information about a family, what categories of information should I make sure to cover?

3. What information should action steps include?

4. What are some common barriers parents may face when addressing their needs? How can I approach these barriers?

5. What are some important things to keep in mind when doing a cost-benefit analysis?

Adam Stein

Lisa Hunter Romanelli

Serene Olin

Geraldine Burton

Group Management Skills

Group Development

Group participation can be an important part of parents' journey toward empowerment. An effective group has the potential to provide parents with motivation and social support, connect parents to similar others in their community, give parents a place to share their experiences, and generate political power for systematic change. As a parent advisor, you should understand that involving parents in a community of peers can have many benefits that go beyond your one-to-one work with each family. Being part of a larger community affords parents the opportunity of meeting others who have "come through the trenches." Parents can share and learn through one another's experiences and, in the process, empower one another with shared knowledge and successes. This experience can offer an important sense of camaraderie and validation to families, who often feel isolated and frustrated in their efforts of advocating for their special needs children across various systems. Being a part of a successful family support group can be critical to making a family feel effective and motivated.

Because of these invaluable benefits, parent advisors should look for opportunities to involve parents with other parents. One of the best means of involving parents with other parents is through groups. Yet running a successful group to achieve these kinds of outcomes is challenging. Running a successful group requires a different skill set than working individually with parents. It involves addressing the needs of the group as a whole and managing group processes to create a safe environment for productive sharing and growth.

This chapter covers different types of groups that parent advisors may run, critical issues to keep in mind when designing a group, stages of group process, and tips for group facilitation.

Types of Groups

There are many different types of groups. Some types of groups you may encounter include parent management groups, consciousness-raising groups, social action groups, social support groups, and skills groups. Table 6.1 provides a brief description of some of the types of groups parent advisors may facilitate.

Remember that each group will differ depending on the type and purpose of the group. For instance, a social action group may be formed to address a specific problem and will exist only until the problem is solved. A parent

Table 6.1 *Different Types of Groups*

Group Type	Characteristics
Parent management groups	■ Directed towards helping parents to develop their parenting skills ■ Parents may be mandated to participate by court order
Consciousness-raising groups	■ Members share experiences and explore feelings about their status (e.g., as parents of children with disabilities) ■ Members explore avenues to empowerment
Social action groups	■ Directed towards bringing about change in the larger environment ■ Task/Issue oriented
Social support groups	■ Directed towards decreasing feelings of isolation ■ Members provide mutual support ■ Members receive help in seeking needed resources
Skills groups	■ Directed towards development of empowerment skills (e.g. leadership, communication, networking)

support group, on the other hand, may be open ended and last for many months or even years with new members coming through all the time.

Getting a Group off the Ground

In general, it is not a good idea to start a group without a stated purpose or to have a group that tries to serve multiple purposes. However, our experience suggests that many parent advisors do so out of necessity because they are often asked or expected to run parent groups without clear direction on what kind of group to start.

The following are some suggestions to keep in mind when you are designing a group in order to increase the likelihood of getting it off the ground.

1. *Conduct a needs assessment.*
   This can be done formally through a survey or informally by word of mouth. Either way, in conducting the needs assessment, you want to try to find out some characteristics of the parent/caregivers in your particular setting. The following are some broad questions you can try to answer through your needs assessment:
   - Are there any specific groups of parents that might form natural support groups (such as grandparents, single parents, or young parents)?
   - Are there any common problems that parents from your agency/organization are dealing with (such as transportation problems with the school district, lack of after-school programs, or respite care)?
   - Are there parents who are looking to get more involved in social action on behalf of children with special needs?
   Once specific needs are determined, outreach for groups can be targeted to specific parents.
2. *Be clear and specific about the group's purpose.*
   Typically, the clearer you can be about the purpose of the group, the more likely it will be successful. For example, a general support group for any parent with a child with mental illness might be appropriate. However, a support group on child management issues might be more effective if groups are targeted at parents with children of similar ages (e.g., preschoolers or adolescents) or specific disorders (e.g., depression or attention-deficit/hyperactivity disorder).
3. *Targeted outreach versus global outreach is preferable.*
   For example, say you are starting a new group for grandparents of children with drug-related conduct problems. Instead of sending a flyer to *all* parents, it would be more effective to generate a list of grandparents who

fit the group's focus (possibly identified through your needs assessment). You can then send flyers to just that list and follow up with phone calls.

4. *Do an individualized initial assessment of challenges and obstacles for each participant.*

Remember your engagement, listening, and priority-setting skills. Ask participants or potential participants about past experiences with the type of group you are forming as well as the mental health system. Elicit their fears, concerns, and questions about what will happen in the group. You should also ask participants about their overall mental or physical health to consider possible accommodations that might be needed.

5. *Take care of the logistics and concrete needs.*

Parents will be more likely to attend groups if the following issues are addressed in advance:

- Time
- Transportation
- Food
- Child care

6. *Make activities fun, engaging, and meaningful.*

- Plan for celebrations
- Have an array of activities (discussion, food, and family time)
- Validate and appreciate participation

Understanding Overall Group Processes

Regardless of the kind of group you are starting, all groups follow a similar developmental process. B. Tuckman, a group development expert, identified five stages of group development: (a) forming, (b) storming, (c) norming, (d) performing, and (e) adjourning. The brief description provided here is not intended to be a comprehensive review of group processes. Rather, its purpose is to point out that certain group processes (e.g., conflict) are normal and can be expected.

The following stages are adapted from Tuckman (1965) and Tuckman and Jensen (1977).

Stage 1: Forming

- Group members rely on the group leader for guidance and direction.
- Group members desire acceptance from the group and have a need to know that the group is safe.

- Group members note similarities and differences with other members and form preferences for future subgroups.
- Rules of behavior seem to keep things simple and avoid controversy. Serious topics and feelings are avoided.
- Members attempt to become oriented to the tasks as well as to one another.
- Discussion centers around defining the scope of the task, how to approach it, and similar concerns.
- To grow from this stage to the next, each member must give up the comfort of nonthreatening topics and risk the possibility of conflict.

Stage 2: Storming

- This stage is characterized by competition, conflict, and organization.
- Individuals have to bend and mold their feelings, ideas, attitudes, and beliefs to suit the group organization.
- During this stage, there will be an increased desire for clarification and commitment.
- Because of the discomfort generated during this stage, some members may remain completely silent, while others attempt to dominate.
- To grow from this stage, group members must move to a problem-solving mentality. The most important trait in helping groups to move on to the next stage seems to be the ability to listen.

Stage 3: Norming

- Relationships in the group are characterized by cohesion.
- Group members actively seek and acknowledge each others' contributions. They seek community building and maintenance as well as group problem solving.
- Members are willing to change their preconceived ideas or opinions on the basis of facts presented by other members.
- Leadership is shared, and cliques dissolve.
- Members build trust and cohesion as they begin to know and identify with one another.
- Members begin to experience a sense of group belonging and a feeling of relief as a result of resolving interpersonal conflicts.
- The major drawback of this stage is that members may begin to fear the inevitable future breakup of the group and may resist change of any sort.

Stage 4: Performing

- This stage is not reached by all groups but is the most productive stage.
- If group members are able to evolve to this stage, personal relations become interdependent.
- In this stage, people can work independently, in subgroups, or as a total unit with equal facility.
- Individual members have become self-assured, and the need for group approval is past.
- There is unity: group identity is complete, group morale is high, and group loyalty is intense.
- There is support for experimentation in solving problems and an emphasis on achievement.
- The overall goal is productivity through problem solving and work.

Stage 5: Adjourning

- Adjourning is the final stage of group development.
- This stage involves the termination of the group.
- A planned conclusion usually includes recognition for participation and achievement and an opportunity for members to say personal good-byes.
- Concluding a group can create some apprehension—in effect, a minor crisis.
- The most effective interventions in this stage are those that facilitate termination and the separation process.

Group Management Tips

It is important for you to learn practical skills for managing a group. Without proper preparation and planning, running a group can be disastrous. The following tips can help you run a successful group. These tips are general guidelines and will vary depending on the group; for example, agendas and specific objectives for each meeting would be less important for a support group than for a task-oriented social action group.

Prepare for the Meeting

- Clearly identify the purpose and objectives of the meeting.
- Anticipate what the participants will and should expect.
- Construct a realistic agenda with high-priority items first.

- Decide how much time will be required and the best time and place for the meeting.
- Make any necessary room and equipment arrangements.
- Notify participants of the purpose, time, and place of the meeting.

Contract

- At the first meeting, establish guidelines or rules that all group members agree to follow.
- You may want to put these guidelines in writing and have each member sign a contract.
- Make sure the group guidelines are prominently posted at each group meeting.

Tips for Getting Started

- Make sure that all participants are introduced to one another.
- Explain the purpose of the discussion and its relevance to the participants.
- A common and effective group process is a "check-in" with group members about their mental or physical state coming into group.
- Briefly present the agenda for the meeting (distribute copies or display where everyone can see).

Keep the Discussion Orderly, Efficient, and Productive

- Distribute materials needed for the discussion (e.g., agendas, fact sheets, and so on).
- Make sure the purpose of the meeting is understood by all.
- Be alert to extended departures from the topic. If the group is drifting away from the topic, call this to everyone's attention. Ask if the digression means that there is disagreement about the goal or purpose of the meeting or if it is an indication that the group is ready to move on to a new topic.
- If there is much repetition in the discussion, ask if the group has exhausted the subject at hand. If so, help them get started on a new topic (e.g., "Does anyone have anything new they would like to add about _____?" "Okay, what are your feelings/experiences with _____?")
- Be the group's timekeeper. Keep the group informed of the time limits so that high-priority topics will get the attention they deserve. As time goes on, you as the group leader can delegate this task to group members in order to share the power.

Give All Members an Equal Opportunity to Participate

- Address your comments and questions to the group as a whole.
- Make sure that all members have a chance to participate.
- Scan the group looking for indications that a member wants to speak (e.g., person is mumbling or making eye contact with you).
- If members of the group dominate the discussion, try some of the following techniques:
    1. When a question is asked of the group, meet the eyes of those members who have spoken infrequently.
    2. When a frequent talker has made a point, ask the group, "How do the rest of you feel?"
    3. In private, ask the excessive talkers to help in getting the quiet members to speak more often. For example, you can call or ask that member to stay after group and say, "Can you help me with some suggestions to get others to share in group?"
    4. Point out the problem and ask others to contribute more. For example, "We have heard a lot from John and Lisa, but what do the rest of you think about _____?"
- If asked by a member to express a personal opinion about a controversial issue, try to bounce the question back to the group.
- Do not comment after each member has spoken; it is too easy to get into a "wheel" pattern of communication, with the leader becoming the hub of the wheel.
- React to what members say with acceptance and without judgment, showing that a point is understood or needs clarification.

Promote Cooperation and Harmony

- Emphasize the importance of the mutual sharing of ideas and experiences and the need for clear communication.
- Use the word "we" often to stress the group's unity of purpose.
- Keep conflicts focused on facts and issues. Stop any personal attacks.

Encourage Critical Thinking

- Ask for more detail and specification.
- Dig for the rationale and assumptions behind an opinion or belief.
- Help those offering opinions to furnish evidence behind the positions they take.

Self-Study

After reviewing this chapter, ask yourself the following questions:

1. What are some things I can do to get a group off the ground?

2. What are the five stages of group development?

3. What should I do if group members drift away from a topic and start talking about issues I am not prepared to discuss?

4. What are some ways to make sure that all members of a group have a chance to participate?

5. What are some techniques I can use with those who dominate the discussion?

Part II

Assisting Parents in Navigating the Mental Health System

7

Getting a Mental
Health Evaluation

Lisa Hunter Romanelli

James Rodriguez

Geraldine Burton

Adam Stein

An accurate assessment is the first step in securing appropriate mental health treatment for a child. Parents may need your guidance in helping them decide the proper venue for an assessment based on their child's needs and circumstances. Parents should be given the most up-to-date information to facilitate their ability to make good decisions and guide their child's mental health care. Accessing the mental health system begins by understanding the key players and what services they can offer. Parents can avoid much delay by knowing what types of assessment services are available and how they will go about finding answers. In order to assist parents, you will need a well-developed practical understanding of assessments and who can conduct them. This chapter provides practical information on mental health assessments and key points for preparing parents in this process.

What Is a Mental Health Assessment?

A mental health assessment is a general description for the various methods used to identify and/or gauge a person's psychological well-being. A mental health assessment can range from a brief interview to an in-depth evaluation with testing. It is important to know that not all mental health assessments yield the same type of information. The results depend on the type of mental health assessment and the qualifications of the individual conducting the assessment. Table 7.1 describes the most common types of mental health assessments and the professionals who typically conduct them. Although each of these assessments is presented individually, it is common for a group of assessments to be administered together during a full evaluation.

Table 7.1 **Types of Assessment**

Type of Assessment	Description	Conducted By
Mental status exam	Briefly evaluates an individual's thinking, feeling, sensing, and perceiving. Common questions include: What is today's date? Where are you? What is your mood today?	Psychiatrist Psychologist Social worker
Diagnostic interview	A structured interview given to determine whether an individual meets the diagnostic criteria for a psychiatric disorder	Psychiatrist Psychologist
Psychological evaluation	Includes an interview, observation, and psychological testing	Psychologist
Psychiatric evaluation	Includes a mental status exam and interview	Psychiatrist
Psychosocial evaluation	Presents an overview of an individual's psychiatric history, family history, developmental history, and interpersonal functioning	Social worker Psychologist

Who Can Conduct Mental Health Assessments?

Who can conduct a mental health assessment may be different in each community. Although psychiatrists, psychologists, and social workers are the most likely to conduct a mental health assessment, a variety of other professionals can make a preliminary assessment of a child's mental health (see Table 7.2).

Where Can You Go to Get a Mental Health Assessment?

Table 7.3 illustrates locations in which you may find providers who can perform a complete or preliminary mental health assessment for a child. The information provided in this chart is based on general locations of providers; situations in your specific area may vary. Preliminary assessments or screens may be available at a variety of locations. More comprehensive mental health assessments, however, are typically found in specialty mental health settings and conducted by professionals with specialized mental health training (see Table 7.1).

Table 7.2 *Types of Professionals*

Type of Professional	Description
School/guidance counselors	School-based professionals who provide educational and supportive counseling to students. Can identify students in need of more specialized mental health services and conduct functional behavioral assessments.
Family doctors (M.D.)	Medical doctors who treat general physical conditions in children, adolescents, and adults. Some family doctors are experienced in prescribing medication for uncomplicated emotional and behavioral problems.
Psychiatric nurse practitioners	Nurse practitioners with specialized mental health training. Typically found in psychiatric hospitals or psychiatric outpatient clinics.
Pediatricians (M.D.)	Medical doctors who specialize in the treatment of children and adolescents. Some pediatricians are experienced in prescribing medication for uncomplicated emotional and behavioral problems.
Physician assistants	Health care professionals licensed to practice medicine under the supervision of a physician. Physician assistants typically do not have specific mental health training but may be able to provide ongoing medication care for simple cases.
Psychiatrists (M.D.)	Medical doctors with special training in the diagnosis and treatment of mental health problems. Can prescribe medication.
Neurologist (M.D.)	Medical doctor with specialized training in the diagnosis and treatment of the nervous system, including the brain. Some neurologists have additional certification in child and adolescent psychiatry. Can prescribe medication.
Clinical psychologists (Ph.D. or Psy.D.)	Mental health experts who hold a doctoral degree and are trained in the diagnosis and treatment of mental health problems. Can conduct psychological testing.

continued

Type of Professional	Description
Licensed clinical social worker/master in social work (LCSW/LMSW)	Licensed mental health experts who hold a master's degree and are trained to provide counseling, case management, or supportive services to children and adults with mental health problems. Cannot prescribe medication or conduct psychological testing.
School psychologists (masters level or Ph.D.)	Certified professionals with special training in psychology and education. They can conduct evaluations to determine social-emotional development and mental health status. They can also provide psychological and crisis counseling for interpersonal or family problems that interfere with school performance. Most work in schools but may be found in a variety of settings.

To find locations that provide mental health assessments for children, parents may begin by asking their child's pediatrician or family doctor for a referral. Numerous Web sites also provide useful information (see Appendix A). One good source is Mental Health America, a leading nonprofit organization with affiliates across the country. It provides links, information, referrals, and other resources for accessing mental health care. This organization can be accessed at www.mentalhealthamerica.net.

Preparing Parents for the Assessment Process

As a parent advisor, part of your job is to prepare parents for what they can expect during the assessment process.

Making the First Call/Initial Contact

It is important to inform parents that the provider or agency intake worker usually will not be able to talk when they first call to get help. They should be prepared to leave a name and phone number so that the call can be returned. Keep in mind that parents often feel uncomfortable or embarrassed about asking for help. This may make it difficult for them to remember everything they want to say when calling an agency or provider. Before they make that first call, help parents make a list of statements and questions to use as a guide.

Table 7.3 *Locations of Providers*

		Locations							
	Outpatient Walk-in Mental Health Clinic	Inpatient Mental Health Clinic	School (General)	School-Based Health Clinic	School-Based Mental Health Clinic	Parent/Family Resource Centers	Family Medical Office	Hospital	Diagnostic Centers
Providers									
School counselors and guidance counselors			X						
Doctors (M.D.s)	X	X	X	X	X		X	X	
Nurse practitioners	X	X	X	X	X		X	X	
Pediatricians	X	X	X	X	X		X	X	
Physicians assistants	X	X	X	X			X	X	
Psychiatrists	X	X	X	X	X			X	
Psychologists	X	X	X	X	X			X	X
Social workers	X	X	X		X	X		X	X

- Prepare a brief description of your child, including his or her problems and why you are seeking help.

- Be ready to supply background information about your family and its members, such as who lives with the child and the ages and marital status of all members of the family.

- Ask whether the provider or agency has time now or in the near future to do an evaluation to see whether treatment is needed.

- If treatment is recommended, will the agency or provider be able to schedule it in the near future?

- When can the first appointment be made? With whom will you talk? How long will the appointment take? Which members of the family should come to the first session?

- What is the fee? Does the agency or provider accept Medical Assistance or payments from your insurance company? Will the Medical Assistance or insurance payments cover the agency's or provider's fee? Will it cover an evaluation if necessary? If you do not have Medical Assistance or private insurance, does the agency or provider offer a sliding-fee scale, or will it obtain funding for you?

Remind parents to always keep in mind their primary concern. It may be easy for them to lose sight of this given the amount of questions that may not be directly related to the main issue.

"Who Is My Doctor?"

Be sure to prepare parents that the first person they meet in most settings may not be the person who will ultimately treat their child. This first person usually conducts what is called an "intake" interview. This interview usually involves asking parents to give a history of their child's development and difficulties. This information is used to determine if their child is eligible for services and to assign the child to an ongoing provider if needed. In a comprehensive mental health evaluation, it is not uncommon for the child to be seen by more than one mental health professional (e.g., psychologist for psychological or educational evaluation and psychiatrist for psychiatric and medication evaluation). One of these providers usually has primary responsibility for the child's overall care.

Waiting for Service

Many agencies, especially community mental health centers, have waiting lists. Prepare parents that they may have to wait for an evaluation, treatment, or both. Unfortunately, the wait may be longer than expected. Parents can become quite discouraged in these situations. It is important to remind parents to contact other similar agencies if the wait is too long. Typically, the first agency can provide contact information for other similar agencies. However, this may not be an option in all regions of the country unless families have private insurance. Some counties may have only one clinic that a child can attend. In this case, it is important for parents to stay connected with you and other parents facing the same circumstances during this stressful time. If the child needs help immediately, encourage parents to let the agency know. If the child is in crisis, they should be sure to say that when making the call. An immediate appointment can usually be arranged in cases of crisis.

Parents' Role in Assessment or Evaluation

Prepare parents for what is expected of them during the intake process. Parents are often asked to meet with the provider first in order to provide background information on their child and family. This information often includes the child's medical history and developmental history (pregnancy, labor, delivery, and early milestones—when child first sat up, walked, talked, and so on).

A description of the child's behavior at home, at school, and in other settings is also obtained. Parents may be uncomfortable answering any questions in front of their child or may need to share something with the clinician that they have not shared with the child. In these cases, they should request a private meeting with the interviewer.

Parents are often asked to complete behavior rating scales and other forms before the first appointment. The information parents provide on these forms helps providers screen for problems. It also helps if parents think about a variety of issues and symptoms related to their child's problem ahead of time. Again, it is important that parents not lose sight of what initially brought them to the intake. This information will help the clinician gain a better understanding and complete picture of the child.

During the first interview, it is important for parents to ask any questions they may have about the intake process. This is also an opportunity for parents to evaluate the clinic's expertise and availability of service. Parents should be encouraged in their role as an equal partner in addressing the needs of the

Highlighting a Child's Strengths and Difficulties

Parents know their child better than anyone else does. They know what their child likes and what he or she does not. They are aware of what that their child does very well and his or her favorable personality traits. Of course, mental health professionals must know the child's difficulties in order to provide the necessary services. It is equally important, however, for them to know the child's strengths in order to have a more complete understanding of the child. In helping parents prepare for the intake interview, the following questions can aid parents in making a list of their child's strengths and difficulties:

- "What does your child do really well?"
- "What things are difficult for your child?"
- "What do other people compliment your child about?"
- "What do other people criticize your child about?"
- "What does your child struggle with?"
- "What comes naturally to your child?"

child and evaluating whether the course of action is suitable for their family. They should come prepared with questions such as the following:

- "How will the assessment be used?"
- "How will my feedback and input be considered in the evaluation?"
- "Will someone fully review the results of the evaluation with me once they are completed?"

Any or all of the assessments listed in Table 7.1 may be conducted at this time. These assessments help the clinician properly diagnose the child.

How Parents Can Prepare Their Child

Most children will feel anxious or upset about being evaluated. This is particularly true if the reason for the evaluation is due to a child's behavior problems or poor school performance. Some children may think that the evaluator is trying to "read their minds." Others may be convinced that they will be punished for their "bad behavior" or problems. Parents must sensitively explain to their child the reason for a mental health evaluation. If the child knows that the parent is supportive and trying to help rather than punish, he or she will be more likely to cooperate and benefit from the evaluation and/or treatment. However, each parent may have a different "comfort zone" about discussing sensitive topics with his or her child. Encourage parents to seek support from you and others in practicing the delivery of information. To begin, parents can help prepare their child by explaining (a) why he or she is being evaluated, (b) what the evaluation will be like, and (c) how the results of the evaluation will be used. Guidelines for each of these steps follow.

Helping the Child Understand Why He or She Is Being Evaluated

In developing an explanation, it will help to remind parents that children are usually aware that they are having trouble in some area (e.g., getting along with peers, crying a lot, controlling temper, or following directions). A parent can begin by telling the child that "*we* have an appointment" (the plural *we* lets the child know that he or she is not alone in this). The parent explains that they will be meeting with a person who can help them figure out why the child is having this problem. (In the case of treatment, this person can help them come up with ways to help make things better for the child in the problem area.) Parents may choose to describe this person (i.e., mental health provider) in different ways. Some parents may choose to avoid the term "doctor" because some children have unpleasant associations with doctors (e.g., needles or shots). Some parents find it helpful to describe the provider as a "counselor," "worry doctor," "feeling doctor," or "talking doctor." If a child has a fear of doctors, it may be helpful for parents to explain the difference between a mental health provider and a typical medical doctor (e.g., "This doctor does not give shots").

Helping the Child Understand What the Evaluation Will Be Like

Parents can help prepare children by explaining the kinds of questions they might be asked. For example, children may be asked about their behaviors, thoughts, or feelings. Younger children may be asked to draw pictures. If a psychological evaluation is expected, parents should be discouraged from using the word "tests." Children tend to associate this to testing in school and can become more anxious. Instead, parents can explain that the psychologist (or "talking doctor" or the child's preferred term) will have the child do some tasks or activities. These tasks can help tell what things the child is good at. They can also help the psychologist better understand why the child is having the problem.

Helping the Child Understand How the Results of the Evaluation Will Be Used

Parents might tell the child that the "talking doctor" (or child's preferred term) will be getting information from the child, parents, teachers, and any other significant caregiver. The psychologist will review this information, together with any other evaluation (e.g., psychological or educational). All this information will be used to help the child, parents, teachers, and the mental health provider (if there is one) understand the problem. It will help everyone involved figure out how to best help the child overcome the problem. It is important that parents assure the child that the results of the evaluation are not used to punish.

Preparing Families to Receive the Assessment Results

Obtaining Feedback

At the end of the evaluation, both the parents and the child will have a chance to hear the results of the evaluation. This is called feedback. It is also an opportunity for the parents to ask questions and to make sure they understand the findings. If parents are afraid that they will not understand the findings or ask the right questions, they can bring someone else (e.g., parent advisor or family friend) along to the feedback session. A good evaluation should provide a balance of the child's (and family's) strengths and weaknesses. Regardless of how severe the child's problems are, a discussion of the child's strengths is important because treatment plans are often designed to take advantage of the child's strong points.

Children also have the right to hear feedback, and this is an important experience for them. An older child may have the feedback given to him or her privately, or the parents may be present if this is agreeable to the child and the evaluator.

Confidentiality

In order for the evaluator to share any information about the evaluation with a third party (e.g., school or insurance company), parents have to agree and sign a release form giving permission to do so. If the evaluation is being conducted for school-related reasons, parents will be asked to sign a release form to allow the results of the evaluation to be communicated to the school. Parents have the right to ask to see what is being communicated to the school beforehand. If parents choose not to sign the release form, the information cannot be shared by the evaluator. Exceptions to this have to do with state laws pertaining to information about the child's safety and the safety of others. These laws can vary from state to state.

Self-Study

After reviewing this chapter, ask yourself the following questions:

1. What are some of the most common types of mental health assessments?

2. Who can conduct a mental health assessment?

3. What are locations in my community that provide mental health assessments?

4. How can I help prepare parents for the mental health assessment process?

5. What can I do to help parents prepare their child for a mental health assessment?

Understanding Psychiatric Diagnoses

Serene Olin

Lisa Hunter Romanelli

Adam Stein

As a parent advisor, it is important to know how mental disorders are diagnosed in children. The diagnostic process can often seem difficult and confusing to parents. The information in this chapter should be used as a resource to help parents understand how diagnostic labels are determined and used. However, diagnosing and treating mental disorders is a complex task, and appropriate training is required. *The material provided in this chapter should be used for informational purposes only.* It is not a substitute for a thorough evaluation or treatment by a licensed mental health provider.

What Is a Psychiatric Diagnosis?

A psychiatric diagnosis is a label for a group of signs and symptoms that characterize a particular psychiatric disorder. There are many different psychiatric diagnoses. All these diagnoses are defined in the American Psychiatric Association's (2000) *Diagnostic and Statistical Manual of Mental Disorders* (text revision; *DSM-IV-TR*), a manual commonly used by mental health professionals. The *DSM-IV-TR* is divided into sections for adults and "disorders usually first evident in infancy, childhood, or adolescence." It is a classification system for understanding and labeling the defining features of childhood mental disorders.

How Do Clinicians Make Psychiatric Diagnoses?

In order to make a psychiatric diagnosis, clinicians first gather information from a variety of sources. Through an interview, the clinician asks the client about his or her thoughts, feelings, behaviors, current experiences, and family history. In the case of children, it is also necessary to gather information from the child's caregivers and teachers. The clinician may also choose to administer diagnostic assessments and conduct psychological testing to assist with the diagnostic process. The clinician uses this information, coupled with the clinician's own impressions, to arrive at a diagnosis. Prior to arriving at a diagnosis, the clinician must make sure of the following:

1. The disorder causes clinically significant distress or impairment in social, occupational, or other important areas of functioning.
2. The disorder is not due to the direct effects of a substance (e.g., alcohol or drugs).
3. The disorder is not due to the direct effects of a general medical condition.

Important Reminders About Psychiatric Diagnoses

The diagnostic process may seem confusing to parents unfamiliar with the mental health system. As a parent advisor, remember that you are not responsible for making diagnoses, but you can help parents understand the process better. Listed next are some important reminders about psychiatric diagnoses to keep in mind when working with parents.

Psychiatric Diagnoses Take Time

In order to make an accurate diagnosis, clinicians must spend a sufficient amount of time gathering information about a child. Parents should be cautious of quick diagnoses that are made on the basis of limited information. For example, they should be careful about accepting a diagnosis made only after a brief meeting or before the clinician has collected information from key caregivers (e.g., teachers) in the child's life. This information is necessary for the clinician to obtain a complete picture of the child's behavior and functioning in different settings.

Psychiatric Diagnoses Should Take a Child's Development Into Account

Depending on a child's age, certain behaviors may be typical and not suggestive of a psychiatric disorder. For example, young children are typically active and have short attention spans. This does not necessarily mean that a young child has attention-deficit/hyperactivity disorder (ADHD). A good psychiatric diagnosis always takes into account a child's developmental stage.

Psychiatric Diagnoses Can Be Wrong

Psychiatric diagnoses are only as good as the clinicians who make them. There are no tests that can absolutely determine whether a child has a specific disorder. Parents should be reminded that if they are uncertain about the accuracy of their child's diagnosis, they should seek a second opinion. Depending on their child's diagnosis, parents may consider getting another consultation at a clinic or center that specializes in the disorder (e.g., an ADHD clinic, a bipolar disorder clinic, or an anxiety clinic). These clinics are often affiliated with university-based hospitals where teams of clinicians have specialized expertise in a given disorder. They can provide a thorough evaluation and a treatment plan, with continuing care provided at clinics more local to the family's home.

What Causes Psychiatric Disorders

When parents first learn that their child has a psychiatric disorder, they often ask why and wonder what caused the disorder. Unfortunately, there is no simple answer to this question. A variety of biological, psychological, and social factors play a role in psychiatric disorders. Many of the resources listed in Appendix A provide more information on specific disorders.

Biological Factors

Genetics: Children with a psychiatric diagnosis are likely to have a parent with the same or a related diagnosis. This suggests that there may be a genetic component to certain psychiatric diagnosis.

Brain Chemicals: Certain brain chemicals called neurotransmitters are associated with some psychiatric disorders. For example, low levels of the neurotransmitter serotonin have been found to contribute to depression.

Medical Conditions: Some medical conditions can cause the same symptoms as psychiatric disorders. For example, hyperthyroidism can cause anxiety symptoms, and some seizure disorders may look like bipolar disorder. It is always important to rule out medical contributors to psychiatric disorders.

Psychological Factors

A variety of psychological factors, such as an individual's personality, thoughts, and beliefs, play a role in the development of a psychiatric disorder. For example, negative thinking contributes to depression.

Social Factors

Stressful life events, such as starting school, moving, or the loss of a parent, can trigger the onset of a psychiatric disorder. Chaotic home environments are also associated with psychiatric disorders. For example, children living in families with parents who fight a lot and use harsh discipline practices are more likely to develop conduct disorder or oppositional defiant disorder (*DSM-IV-TR*).

Diagnostic Labels and Their Implications

Emotional and behavior problems in children carry different labels in different settings. These labels include behaviorally disordered, socially maladjusted, delinquent, psychotic, emotionally handicapped or disturbed, and mentally ill.

Within the educational setting, students with such disorders are categorized as having an emotional disturbance (ED), which is defined under the Individuals with Disabilities Education Improvement Act (Individuals with Disabilities Education Improvement Act (IDEIA); Code of Federal Regulations, Section 300.8[c][4][i]2007) as follows:

> . . . a condition exhibiting one or more of the following characteristics over a long period of time and to a marked degree that adversely affects a child's educational performance
>
> A. An inability to learn that cannot be explained by intellectual, sensory or health factors.
> B. An inability to build or maintain satisfactory interpersonal relationships with peers and teachers.
> C. Inappropriate types of behavior or feelings under normal circumstances.
> D. A general pervasive mood of unhappiness or depression.
> E. A tendency to develop physical symptoms or fears associated with personal or school problems.

As defined by the IDEA, emotional disturbance includes schizophrenia but does not apply to children who are socially maladjusted, unless it is determined that they have an emotional disturbance.

The Department of Education's definition of ED suggests that a broad range of behaviors might result in a child being eligible for special education. Children who qualify for special education may receive psychological services and counseling, as part of their Individual Education Plans (see Chapter 13 for more information).

Problems With Diagnostic Labels

Parent advisors should note that historically, the field of childhood mental health has downplayed diagnosis for a number of reasons (U.S. Department of Health and Human Services, 1999). First, children are rapidly changing so that some behaviors may be quite normal at one age but may indicate a mental disorder at another age.

Second, children are often not able to verbalize their thoughts and feelings or to provide an accurate description of their behavior. Consequently, diagnoses of mental disorders are often based on information provided by parents, teachers, and other caregivers. These individuals may not be the best judge of a child's mental processes.

Third, the criteria for many mental disorders in children are based on adult criteria. This practice of using adult criteria to draw inferences about children is controversial. It can be quite problematic to use adult criteria because the same disorder can be expressed quite differently in children. These differences often contribute to diagnostic uncertainty in children. Despite these issues, the trend for diagnostic labels is increasing. This is in part due to tougher reimbursement standards, the development of practice guidelines, and the development of more appropriate diagnostic categories and criteria.

Diagnostic Label as One Piece of the Puzzle

It is helpful to remind parents that a diagnosis is only one part of a mental health evaluation. A good evaluation also addresses the child's problem in context of his or her personal situation. Children's dependence on their caregivers makes them vulnerable to multiple influences over which they have little control (e.g., parents' mental health, marital function, family dynamics, and school or neighborhood environment). These influences affect the nature and severity of the impairment associated with the disorder. They also affect how treatment progresses and whether treatment gains are maintained. In addition, the child's symptoms also affect the family. Understanding children's diagnoses within the context of their environments is key in the successful treatment of childhood mental disorders.

Pros and Cons of Diagnostic Labels

In discussing diagnostic labels with parents, parent advisors can keep in mind the pros and cons of this practice.

Pros

Provides Relief to Families: Some parents spend a long time struggling to figure out their child's problems. A diagnostic label can provide some relief by putting a name to the difficulties their child and family have been dealing with.

Tool for Communication: Diagnostic labels provide a common language for mental health professionals to talk about mental disorders.

Facilitates Research: Diagnostic labels are useful in scientific research and surveillance studies (studies that track people or groups of people). They allow people with similar conditions to be grouped together and studied.

Necessary for Reimbursement or Services: Many insurance and managed care companies typically require a *DSM* diagnosis for reimbursement of services. Schools require an ED label to qualify for mental health services.

Guide to Appropriate Treatment: At a larger level, diagnoses allow clinicians and researchers to develop practice guidelines for disorders that can help standardize treatment. At an individual level, a diagnosis can help determine the type of treatment. Diagnoses can help identify children who may respond well to treatments that have been found to be safe and effective for other children with similar problems.

Cons

Stigma: Lack of understanding and misconceptions about mental illness are widespread and contribute to stigma. As a result, parents may be reluctant to get help. They may be concerned about discrimination. Parents may fear that being diagnosed with a mental disorder could influence their child's school or vocational options. In some cultures, parents may worry about shame on the family. Children may be concerned about getting teased by peers.

Limits View of Mental Disorders in Children: A diagnostic label alone does not provide a complete picture. It does not tell us about how the child is functioning or his or her level of impairment in various settings.

Risk of Misdiagnosis: Misdiagnosis can have grave consequences. Parents should be encouraged to obtain second or more opinions if they are concerned that their child has been misdiagnosed.

Impact of Culture and Ethnicity on Psychiatric Diagnoses and Obtaining Services

Different cultures express and report distress differently (U.S. Department of Health and Human Services, 2001). Culture affects how people explain the causes of mental health problems, how they perceive treatment providers, and how they respond to interventions. Cultural meanings of illness have real consequences. How people understand their problems influences how motivated they are to seek help and how they cope with their symptoms. It also affects how supportive their families and communities are and where they are willing to go for help. These factors in turn influence how well they fare in treatment.

Assessment tools that are currently used are often not able to capture key signs and symptoms associated with common mental illnesses. For example, some languages do not have words for "depressed" and "anxious." Further, some minority parents may not speak English. As a result, mental health evaluations are often conducted in another language or are dependent on translations. This can be problematic for an accurate diagnosis.

Aside from obvious language issues, other factors affecting minority populations also serve as real barriers to obtaining help. Because of historical and sociocultural factors in the United States, many minority groups do not trust psychiatric labels or the medical profession. Further, mental illness continues to carry a strong sense of stigma. Parents may be reluctant to have their child labeled in order to obtain needed services.

Parent advisors should directly address these important issues with parents as appropriate. They can provide a sounding board for such families to discuss their fears, correct misperceptions, and receive reassurance. Parent advisors can also help parents strategize ways to communicate their concerns directly to their provider.

Self-Study

After reviewing this chapter, ask yourself the following questions:

1. What is a psychiatric diagnosis?

2. What are some important things to remember about psychiatric diagnoses in children?

3. What are some factors that contribute to psychiatric disorders?

4. What does "ED" stand for, and why is it important to know?

5. What are some pros and cons of diagnostic labels?

6. How does culture influence parents' approach to mental health care?

Lisa Hunter

Serene Olin

Geraldine Burton

Polly Gipson

Adam Stein

Considering Mental
Health Treatments

O nce a child has been evaluated, a treatment is usually recommended. As a parent advisor, you should be familiar with common treatments for mental disorders. You will also find it hopeful to be knowledgeable about the different mental health service delivery options. This chapter presents basic information on the types of treatment available. It also provides tables summarizing many of the service delivery options.

What Kind of Help Is Available?

As part of the mental health evaluation, parents should be provided with information about the types of interventions that may be helpful to their child's problem. This should include the kinds of treatment that have been used or studied in children with similar diagnoses. The rationale for each type of intervention should be clearly explained. Parents should be informed of the risks and benefits of each treatment. They should also understand how a treatment might be relevant to their situation.

In general, interventions can be classified as involving *psychosocial treatments* (also known as psychotherapy or talk therapy) or *medications* (also known as pharmacological interventions). In addressing child mental disorders, psychosocial treatments are usually tried first. This is due to the low risk associated with such interventions. In treating children and adolescents with mental disorders, experts generally agree that medications should *not* be the only strategy used to address these problems. Psychosocial interventions can teach skills that can help the child and family maintain treatment benefits when medications are withdrawn.

In helping parents seek appropriate treatment for their child, you may encounter the phrase "evidence-based practice." This phrase is generally used in two ways:

1. To describe the integration of clinical expertise with the best research evidence available to patient care
2. To describe specific interventions that have been tested and shown to consistently produce specific and predictable outcomes for an identified problem

There is currently a good scientific knowledge base for treatments for children and adolescents with mental disorders. However, not all disorders and treatments have been researched to the same degree. That does not mean treatments for which there is currently no evidence base are bad or wrong. The reality is that scientifically validated interventions do not exist for every condition or every type of population. Further, not all evidence-based treatments work for all people. Even if the individual has similar diagnoses, symptoms, or situations as the population that was studied, the treatment may have different outcomes. Yet parents are likely to be reassured that the treatments their child are receiving have some evidence of effectiveness. Skilled providers use their expertise flexibly to integrate clinical care with the best available scientific knowledge in order to meet the unique needs of individuals.

Psychosocial Treatments

These interventions may be focused on the child, the family, or the child's environment. Different types of psychosocial interventions are commonly used to treat child mental disorders. Interventions may include the following:

- Behavior management
- Parent training
- Improving relationships with peers and family members
- Changing negative thoughts, feelings, and behaviors
- Exposure to fears or worries
- Developing coping strategies

- Social skills training
- Anger management

Pharmacological Interventions

There are several major categories of psychotropic medications used in children and adolescents: stimulants, antidepressants, antianxiety agents, antipsychotics, and mood stabilizers.

Stimulant Medications: These medications are used to treat attention-deficit/hyperactivity disorder, the most common behavioral disorder of childhood. Stimulant medications have been extensively studied and are specifically labeled for pediatric use.

Antidepressant and Antianxiety Medications: After stimulants, these are the next most commonly prescribed medications in children and adolescents. They are used for depression and anxiety disorders. The medications most widely prescribed for these disorders are selective serotonin reuptake inhibitors (commonly referred to as SSRIs).

Antipsychotic Medications: These medications are used to treat children with schizophrenia, bipolar disorder, autism, Tourette's syndrome, and severe conduct disorders. Their use requires close monitoring for side effects.

Mood-Stabilizing Medications: These medications are used to treat bipolar disorder (manic-depressive illness). However, because there are very limited data on the safety and efficacy of most mood stabilizers in youth, treatment of children and adolescents is mainly based on experience with adults. The most frequently used mood stabilizers are lithium and valproate (Depakote®). Their use requires close monitoring for side effects.

Mental Health Service Delivery Options

Parents will regularly seek your guidance about where their child can receive mental health services. It is important for you to be fully aware of the mental health service system in your communities. The following tables can be used to familiarize yourself with the service delivery options offered in many hospitals and clinics throughout the country, specifically, outpatient services, inpatient services, residential and nonresidential services, and emergency services.

Outpatient Services

A child goes to outpatient services for treatment but does not live or spend the night at such facilities. Clinic treatment and day treatment are examples of such services. Your pediatrician's office may also be a source of outpatient services, especially for young children under the age of 5 (see Table 9.1).

Table 9.1 *Types of Outpatient Services*

Clinic treatment	<ul><li>Usually staffed with psychologists, psychiatrists, social workers, and other professionals.</li><li>Offers a variety of services including individual therapy, group therapy, family therapy, and medication management.</li><li>Treatment sites may be within a child's school, community hospital, or a provider's private office.</li><li>Treatment can be accessed independently or through the school psychologist.</li></ul>
Day treatment	<ul><li>Available only with a referral from the board of education.</li><li>Useful for children who need treatment throughout the day.</li><li>Combination of treatment and educational services that address the child's mental health needs in small classroom settings within public schools or through separate programs.</li><li>Offers individual therapy, group therapy, family therapy, and medication management.</li><li>Provides some combination of art, music, and drama therapy.</li></ul>

Nonresidential Community Supports

These community support services are for families whose children are living at home (see Table 9.2).

Table 9.2 *Types of Nonresidential Community Supports*

Family network	▪ Many states have family networking processes available for families that bring together all those involved with a child's treatment, such as mental health service providers, parent advisors, teachers, and family members. ▪ Goal is to develop a plan for the child's treatment in which all involved have an equal voice.
Parent support centers/ family support programs	▪ Agencies or centers that offer parent-to-parent education, advocacy, and support services in which the staff are parents of children with emotional or behavioral disturbances. ▪ Staff may accompany parents to a variety of appointments including but not limited to mental health services (e.g., human resources administration or juvenile court). ▪ Staff is well informed about the services and programs available in the community.
Respite care	▪ Trained workers provide families with a temporary break from caring for a child with special needs. ▪ This service can be arranged for a few hours or days and may take place in or out of the home. ▪ Gives parents an opportunity to handle routine tasks or to relax. ▪ Available for children ages 5 to 18 years. ▪ All requests must be made by a professional associated with the child and his or her family.
Intensive case management	▪ Publicly funded program offered by a community or hospital provider to reduce the need for inpatient admission, shorten residential placement, and prevent emergency room visits. ▪ Serves children and adolescents between the ages of 5 and 18 with a history of psychiatric hospitalizations or residential care or at risk for an out-of-home placement.

continued

	▪ Provides a specially trained child mental health provider who is available 24 hours a day, 7 days a week, to work with families to coordinate the services and supports needed to keep the child at home. ▪ Referrals can be made by psychiatric hospitals, residential programs, community mental health providers, and families themselves.
Home- and community-based waiver	▪ Goal is to keep children at home with their families even when the child is eligible for inpatient services or placement in a residential treatment facility. ▪ Waives parental income and makes the child eligible for Medicaid. ▪ Provides a waiver to use the money that would pay for a residential program to pay for services to keep the child at home (e.g., respite care, skills training to assist the child and family to live together, individualized care coordination, and crisis response). ▪ Available to children from age 5 until 18th birthday (children who enter waiver by 18 can receive services until 21). ▪ Referrals can be made by parents or a representative of any child serving system. ▪ Families are expected to use services for approximately 9 months.
Miscellaneous community supports	▪ Family support services, vocational services, after-school therapeutic, recreational and tutorial programs, home care, and self-help groups. ▪ A list of programs can be obtained through family resource centers and your city or state department of mental health.

Residential Community Supports

These services are offered to families when it is no longer possible for their children to continue living at home (see Table 9.3).

Table 9.3 *Types of Residential Community Supports*

Community residences	▪ Small group homes that serve six to eight children who live with and are supervised by trained staff. ▪ Provide a structured living environment that includes daily living activities, problem-solving training, and behavior management skills training. ▪ Participation in the community in which the residence is located is key—children attend local neighborhood schools and participate in local recreation and cultural activities. ▪ Treatment services are provided by local mental health providers as well as residence staff. ▪ Ages vary according to specific residences (i.e. 5–12, 11–16, and so on).
Family-based treatment	▪ Service offered in special homes with "professional parents" trained to work with the mental health needs of children and their families. ▪ Differs from foster parents in that parents do not have to give up legal custody of their child to be a part of this program. ▪ Assigns a family specialist in addition to the professional parents who works with all parties involved in the child's treatment. ▪ Offers a combination of programs, such as behavior management, independent living skills training, counseling, medication management, and other family support services. ▪ Available to children ages 5 to 16 through referral by psychiatric hospitals, residential treatment facilities, or a variety of other referring sources, depending on state mandates and processes.

Inpatient Services

These services are for children who require hospitalization because of their mental health needs (see Table 9.4).

Table 9.4 **Types of Inpatient Services**

Acute care	▪ Necessary when a child has become dangerous either to him- or herself or to others. ▪ The child will be admitted to a local hospital. ▪ Usually provided in separate units reserved for children. ▪ Usually required for a few days to a few weeks. ▪ Doctor may recommend this option to monitor a child's behavior or symptoms, to test new medications, or to make a judgment about a diagnosis. ▪ Referrals are made by a doctor.
Intermediate care	▪ Necessary when a child requires a longer hospitalization stay. ▪ Doctor may move the child from acute care to a hospital that provides this level of care. ▪ Usually these services are available in state children's psychiatric hospitals. ▪ Referrals are made by a doctor.
Residential treatment facilities	▪ Necessary when a child requires care for at least 180 days or more. ▪ Serve children between the ages of 6 and 21 years and with an IQ over 50. ▪ Provide schooling within the grounds of the facility. ▪ Referrals can be made by family, psychiatric hospitals, community mental health providers, Child Protective Services (CPS), or committees on special education. ▪ All referrals must be reviewed by committees that oversee eligibility.

Emergency Services

Emergency services are necessary when a parent needs immediate help (see Table 9.5). If a child is at risk of hurting him- or herself or others, advise parents that the best thing to do is dial 911 (see Table 9.5).

Table 9.5 *Types of Emergency Services*

Crisis respite program	▪ Provides a brief placement from 5 to 12 days with a professional parent. ▪ Goal is to prevent the child from being placed outside the home for an even longer period. ▪ Not required for parents to give up legal custody for this program. ▪ For children ages 5 to 18. ▪ Referrals made by a mental health professional familiar with the child and family.
Extended observation beds	▪ Short-term observation and evaluation up to 72 hours in a hospital. ▪ Usually hospital staff recommends longer hospitalization or that the child be returned home, depending on the nature of the visit.
Mobile crisis teams	▪ Provides a team of professionals, which may include a psychiatrist, psychiatric nurse, and/or social worker, who visit a family's home to make recommendations for the next steps to take for the child.
Home-based crisis intervention services	▪ In-home services for children and adolescents between the ages of 5 and 18 who are believed to be at risk for psychiatric hospitalization. ▪ Intensive services are provided for 4 to 6 weeks in the child's home or in other familiar settings, such as school. ▪ Service includes crisis intervention, behavioral skills training, behavior management, and individual and family counseling. ▪ Referral required by an emergency room, walk-in clinic, or a mobile crisis team.

continued

	▪ Only referrals from designated sources that include a mental status evaluation signed by a psychiatrist stating that the child is being referred in lieu of hospitalization will be considered.
Hospital psychiatric emergency rooms	▪ Facilities that are similar to rooms used in a physical or medical emergency but intended for psychiatric or behavioral emergencies. ▪ Not all hospitals have psychiatric emergency rooms or psychiatric emergency rooms for children. ▪ Local hospitals, the child's treating clinic, or mental health provider can offer information on the nearest psychiatric emergency rooms in your area.
Walk-in clinics	▪ Facilities that offer immediate but not emergency care. ▪ No appointment is required. ▪ Not all walk-in clinics offer psychiatric care for adults or children.

Service Delivery Options

As described in the previous section, parents have a variety of options when seeking mental health services for their child. Sometimes it may be difficult for parents to determine which service is best for their child's current issues. Remind parents to call 911 or a local hotline if a child is an immediate danger to him- or herself or others. Most other mental health needs can be served by using resources in your community.

Self-Study

After reviewing this chapter, ask yourself the following questions:

1. What are the two main types of treatment available?

2. What does it mean if a practice is "evidence based"?

3. What is the difference between outpatient and inpatient services?

4. What is the difference between residential and nonresidential community supports?

5. What are some of the emergency mental health services available to parents?

Working With Providers

Serene Olin

Geradline Burton

It is important for parents to work effectively with their child's mental health care provider during treatment. This chapter provides information to help prepare parents for the treatment process. It includes tips to help parents form a productive partnership with providers. Finally, it offers strategies for assertive communication.

Preparing Parents for Treatment

Parent may have many questions when beginning treatment for their child. As a parent advisor, you may need to address the following questions from parents.

"How Long Will Treatment Take, and What Will It Involve?"

Based on the evaluator's formulation of the problem, parents should be provided an estimate of how long treatment may take. They should be given a description of what would be involved (e.g., working with the school, parent training, medication, social skills training for the child, and so on). Parents should work with their evaluator to determine the best possible options. (See Chapter 9 for more information on treatment options.) Based on the recommended treatment, programs may be located at community agencies, hospitals, or private offices. Treatment sessions can vary depending on the type of therapy the child is receiving. Some may involve simply talking or using play as a means of communication. Others may include homework for the child to complete. Additionally, the child's provider may ask parents to take part in some sessions. Parents may also be asked to make some changes to their home life in order to supplement the changes taking place in therapy.

Know Your Child's Medications

- Learn the trade and generic names of the medications

- Keep a list of the medications in a handy place

- Keep records of the names, dates, dosages, and prescribing doctor of all medications

- Learn the purpose of the medications

Know the Potential Side Effects of Your Child's Medication

- Have the doctor list potential side effects

- Take notice of side effects and report them to your doctor

Follow the Doctor's Advice About a Medication

- Make sure your child takes his or her medication only as prescribed

- Find out from your doctor or pharmacist what food or drinks to avoid

- Find out if any activities should be restricted

Safety

- Don't give your child any over-the-counter drugs or any other medication without first checking with your doctor about interactions

- Keep all medication out of the reach of children

- Have an adult supervise your child's intake of medication

- Never give your child's medication to another person or let your child take a medication not prescribed by his or her doctor

- Tell your child's other doctors, including dentists, what medications your child is taking

"What If the Doctor Recommends Medication?"

Many parents have mixed feelings about whether to give their child medication. You also may have mixed feelings about the use of medication for a specific disorder; however, it is important not to let your personal views about medication influence your work with parents. It is more important to provide parents with accurate information and let them make an informed decision for their child's treatment. Remember to encourage parents to discuss medication concerns with their child's doctors. If their child is on medication, parents may also find the tips on page 102 helpful. Remind parents that it is important to manage their child's medication for it to be used safely and effectively.

"How Much Will Treatment Cost?"

Treatment cost should be discussed up front. Parents need to know what the fee is for services ahead of time. How parents pay for their child's services depends on their particular situation, including financial needs and eligibility for certain programs. Important questions to ask include the following:

- Does the agency or provider accept Medical Assistance or payments from the family's insurance company?
- Will the Medical Assistance or insurance payments cover the whole fee?
- If the family does not have Medical Assistance or private insurance, does the provider offer a sliding-fee scale, or will the provider obtain funding for the family?

Parents may also want to explore services available at their child's school. Some children attend schools with school-based mental health clinics that have a variety of services to offer their students.

"What Is Realistic for My Family?"

It is important to have all the information regarding treatment needs, options available, and costs involved. However, parents also need to discuss what is currently realistic for their family. For example, they may need after-hour appointments or child care for other children. Such a discussion can often help avoid early treatment termination or no-shows for appointments. It also helps the family to prioritize their needs and maximize the help they can get.

"How Will I Know If Treatment Is Helping?"

Ongoing monitoring of the child's symptoms and functioning is important in determining whether the treatment is working. The frequency of this monitoring depends on a variety of factors. These may include the type of medication, the target outcomes for treatment, and the severity of the problem. Remind parents that they and their child's provider are partnering to help their child. It is important that parents ask their child's provider any questions they may have about treatment sessions. Encourage parents to speak candidly with their child's provider about what they feel is not working as well as what aspects of the treatment they are pleased with.

Together with their provider(s), parents and their child should determine a few realistic goals for treatment. A few examples are decrease hyperactivity so that the child does not disrupt the classroom, increase attention span so that the child completes 75% of homework, initiate participation in one pleasurable activity, and improve relationships with parents and friends. In assessing the success of the treatment plan, parents and their providers should ask if the target outcomes were met. If so, they should consider how the treatment can be adjusted to further improve target outcomes or maintain treatment gains.

If treatment goals are not being met, the following checklist should be considered:

- Were goals realistic?
- Is more information needed to understand the child's behavior?
- Is the diagnosis accurate?
- Are there other issues or co-occurring conditions affecting treatment?
- Is the treatment plan being followed?

"What Can I Do If I Think the Treatment Isn't Working?"

If parents think treatment is not helping, encourage them to do the following:

- Talk about their concerns or doubts
- Get another opinion or ask for a consultation

It is important to help parents understand that the treatment of mental disorders follows the same principles that are used to treat other chronic disorders, such as diabetes or high blood pressure. Long-term planning is often needed because these conditions recur or continue for a long time. Treatment may not completely get rid of the symptoms. However, treatment should help parents and their child *manage* the disorder on an ongoing basis. Because children continue to develop, treatment plans will likely need adjustments over time.

Principles for Effective Parent–Provider Partnerships

Parent-provider partnerships are essential to a child's treatment. This section presents basic principles for forming effective parent–provider partnerships. As a parent advisor, you can give parents the following tips:

Remember to Participate

An effective parent-provider partnership demands active participation from both parents and providers. You can suggest to parents some ways they can participate in their child's treatment, such as the following sample dialogues:

- *Speak up.* Be vocal and let your providers know that you want to take an active role in your child's treatment. At first, you may find this difficult, but with practice and support, you can learn to approach your provider with ease. If there are questions that are not being addressed during a session (lack of time may be a factor), attempt to schedule a day and time when it can be done.
- *Provide information.* You know a lot about your child but sometimes may not have the opportunity to share your knowledge with your child's provider. Make an effort to tell your child's provider all that you can about your child's history, symptoms, needs, and so on.

Remember That Parents Are Experts, Too!

Parents are the most knowledgeable experts concerning their child. They know their child's development, strengths, assets, and special challenges. They have much more opportunity to know and observe their child than a provider does and can provide valuable information about their child's functioning. Remind parents that they must also get input and advice from others. However, if they are told something that does not fit with their prior experiences, they should ask questions and seek to explain to the health care professional why they feel as they do.

Know Your Limits

In addition to realizing that they too are an expert about their child, parents must also know their limits when it comes to collaborating with their child's provider. Parents should negotiate their role in their child's treatment with their provider. They should be careful not to assume more responsibilities than they are capable of performing. As a parent advisor, you can help parents define their limits and work with their provider.

Recognize Efforts by Professionals

Remind parents that it is important to show their appreciation to their providers. Providers enjoy receiving positive feedback. Such feedback can help establish and maintain a healthy respect and working relationship. After parents finish working with a provider, they should consider keeping in touch. Because of the time-limited involvement that providers typically have with families, they often have no knowledge as to how events have unfolded. They are usually genuinely interested in hearing from former clients.

Get the Facts

Emphasize to parents that it is crucial to get accurate information about their child's condition and treatment. This requires asking a lot of questions. If parents do not understand something a provider has said, they should ask questions until it is clear. A provider will assume that parents understand unless they let him or her know otherwise.

Here are tips to give parents:

- *Take notes.* Writing down what your provider says will help you remember what you need to know about your child's treatment.
- *Make a list of questions.* Asking your provider questions may be difficult at first. Writing down your questions before you meet with your provider will make asking the questions easier.
- *Repeat what you heard.* If you are having a complicated discussion with your provider, it may be helpful to repeat what you heard in your own words. This is a good way of confirming that you understood what the provider said.
- *Keep a file.* Keep all the important documents related to your child's treatment in an easy-to-access file or binder. Review this binder periodically to make sure you have all the important facts related to your child's treatment.
- *Keep a log of contact.* Use this log to keep track of items discussed with your doctor.

How to Communicate Effectively With Providers

Effective communication is a key component to establishing a successful parent-professional partnership. Although some barriers might exist that prevent effective communication, it is possible for parents to learn how to better communicate their feelings. Effectively expressing their frustration, dissatisfaction, or approval will help parents get the most out of mental health services. Parent advisors can help parents improve their interactions with their child's mental health provider by teaching them good communication skills.

Parents sometimes find talking to their child's provider about the treatment process intimidating. When uneasy, most people resort to one of three styles of communication:

> *Passive communicators* keep their feelings to themselves. This often results in giving into others with a sense of inferiority. Ultimately, it may mean allowing others to decide on the services needed.
>
> *Aggressive communicators* attack the person rather than the problem. They exhibit a sense of hostility and a lack of mutual respect.
>
> *Assertive communicators* confront the problem instead of the person. Voicing their feelings, they seek to work toward goals and make their own choices.

The most effective communicator is one who is assertive; however, becoming an assertive communicator takes time and practice. You can give parents the following tips.

Tips for Assertive Communication

- Focus on the problem, not the person.
- Seek solutions, ask questions, and seek clarification. Example: "Could you explain what it means for my child to be diagnosed with attention-deficit/hyperactivity disorder? Also, could you explain it to me as you would to my child so that I can talk to him or her about it?"
- Project that you are someone who is willing to listen and consider the other point of view.
- Use "I" statements to demonstrate ownership of your feelings. Example: "I don't feel comfortable with this diagnosis" versus "Your diagnosis is making me uncomfortable."
- Communicate your feelings without using offensive or accusatory language.
- Establish and maintain eye contact throughout the conversation.
- Direct your face and body toward the person and keep a straight posture.
- Incorporate facial expressions and normal hand gestures to represent your thoughts.
- Maintain a moderate tone and pitch of voice.

Self-Study

After reviewing this chapter, ask yourself the following questions:

1. What are some common questions parents have when their child begins treatment?

2. What are some tips to give parents about managing medication?

3. What can parents do if they do not think the treatment is helping?

4. What are some suggestions I can give parents about partnering with providers?

5. How can I help parents communicate effectively with their providers?

11

Specific Disorders

Lisa Hunter Romanelli

Serene Olin

This chapter reviews some of the most common child mental disorders and their treatments. The specific disorders covered are disruptive behavior disorders (conduct disorder, oppositional defiant disorder, attention-deficit/ hyperactivity disorder), posttraumatic stress disorder and other anxiety disorders (separation anxiety disorder, specific phobias, social phobia, generalized anxiety disorder, panic disorder, obsessive-compulsive disorder), mood disorders (depression and bipolar disorder), and substance abuse. The material in this chapter is based on numerous sources, including the *Diagnostic and Statistical Manual of Mental Disorder* (text revision; *DSM-IV-TR*) (American Psychiatric Association, 2000) and other sources cited within the text.

The information provided in this chapter should be used as an informational resource only. It is not intended as a diagnostic tool. Remember that your job is not to diagnose disorders or recommend treatments but to help parents explore their options and access care. Encourage parents to speak to their child's mental health provider or doctor about their child's diagnosis and treatment options. For more information on these and other disorders, refer to Appendix A of this book. You may also want to keep your own list of resources that you can share with parents.

Disruptive Behavior Disorders

Disruptive behaviors such as hyperactivity, tantrums, talking back to adults, fighting, stealing, and destroying property are the most common reasons parents seek help for their children. These behaviors are difficult to ignore and cause problems for both children and their parents. In this section, we discuss the diagnosis and treatment of three forms of disruptive behavior disorders: conduct disorder, oppositional defiant disorder, and attention-deficit/hyperactivity disorder.

Conduct Disorder

Defining Conduct Disorder: According to the *DSM-IV-TR,* conduct disorder (CD) is characterized by serious aggressive or nonaggressive behaviors toward people, animals, or property. All children and adolescents will occasionally misbehave. Children and adolescents with CD, however, display a pattern of severe and repeated acting-out behavior characterized by the following:

- Bullying or threatening others
- Starting physical fights
- Using a weapon
- Physical cruelty to animals
- Vandalism
- Breaking into the homes or cars of others
- Lying
- Stealing
- Staying out at night without parental permission
- Running away from home overnight
- Frequent truancy from school

Conduct disorder usually begins in late childhood or early adolescence but can develop before age 10. It is much more common in boys than girls. Boys with CD tend to fight, steal, and vandalize property. Girls with CD are more likely to lie, run away, and act out sexually. Both boys and girls with CD are at an extremely high risk for substance abuse and school problems.

Children with CD are often viewed by others as "delinquent" or "bad" rather than mentally ill. As a result, many children with CD do not receive the mental health services they need. Children with CD are sometimes more likely to be incarcerated because of serious conduct problems. Their mental health needs often go untreated.

Diagnosing CD: A diagnosis of CD requires that a child display at least three or more of the behaviors listed previously for one year. When diagnosing CD, mental health professionals speak to parents and teachers and consider the following:

- Are these behaviors serious and long standing?
- How frequently do these behaviors occur?

- Are these behaviors a response to a temporary situation or related to another problem or disorder?
- Do these behaviors significantly interfere with the child's functioning at school or home or with friends?

When diagnosing CD, it is also important for mental health professionals to determine if a child has any other mental health or learning problems. Learning disorders and attention-deficit/hyperactivity disorder are common among youth with CD. Other disorders that may co-occur with CD include depression, bipolar disorder, and substance abuse.

Oppositional Defiant Disorder

Defining Oppositional Defiant Disorder: Oppositional defiant disorder (ODD) is characterized by argumentative, disobedient, stubborn, negative, and defiant behavior toward parents, teachers, and other authority figures. Although some of the behaviors associated with ODD are also seen in CD, ODD is generally less severe than CD. Listed here are some common ODD behaviors:

- Often loses temper
- Often argues with adults
- Often actively defies or refuses to comply with adults' requests or rules
- Often deliberately annoys people
- Often blames others for his or her mistakes or misbehavior
- Often touchy or easily annoyed by others
- Often angry and resentful
- Often spiteful or vindictive

According to the *DSM-IV-TR,* in order to be diagnosed with ODD, a child must display a pattern of defiant behavior that lasts for at least *6 months,* during which *four or more* of the previously listed behaviors are present.

Diagnosing ODD: Oppositional defiant disorder typically begins by age 8 and usually not later than early adolescence. It can be difficult to diagnose because oppositional behavior is a normal part of a child's development. In addition, children may argue, disobey, and defy parents and other adults, particularly when they are tired, under stress, hungry, or upset. In order to assess whether a child has ODD, providers consider the following questions:

- How frequently do these behaviors occur?
- Do these behaviors interfere with the child's functioning at school or home or with friends?
- Are there other things that might be causing these behaviors?

When diagnosing ODD, it is also important for mental health professionals to determine if a child has any other mental health problems. Attention-deficit/hyperactivity disorder and anxiety disorders are common in children with ODD.

Treatments for CD and ODD

A psychosocial intervention is usually the first type of treatment a child diagnosed with CD or ODD receives. Medications are sometimes prescribed for children with CD or ODD who display impulsive aggression (i.e., aggressive behavior that is reactive rather than planned). Information about psychosocial interventions and medications for CD and ODD follows.

Psychosocial Interventions: A wide range of psychosocial interventions have been identified for CD and ODD (see Farmer, Compton, Burns, & Robertson, 2002; *Blueprints for Violence,* www.colorado.edu/cspv/blueprints/index.html). Generally, ODD responds better to treatment than CD, which is difficult to treat and often requires early and long-term intervention. Youth with severe cases of CD may require treatment in a residential setting.

Parent Training

- Educates parents about typical child behavior and teaches them more effective ways to monitor and manage behaviors
- Gives parents opportunities to practice new parenting skills with their child in the presence of a mental health professional

Functional Family Therapy

- Short-term therapy for youths between the ages 11 and 18 who are at risk for delinquency, violence, substance abuse, CD, and ODD
- Helps to improve youth and family communication, interaction, and problem solving
- Helps families to better utilize community resources

Multisystemic Therapy

- Intensive treatment for chronic and violent juvenile offenders
- Targets family, peer, school, and neighborhood factors that contribute to antisocial behavior
- Helps parents to deal more effectively with their child's behavior problems

Cognitive-Behavioral Therapy

- Helps children learn how to identify their feelings and the relationship between feelings, thoughts, and behavior
- Teaches children anger management skills and problem-solving skills

Social Skills Training

- Teaches children how to make friends and resolve conflict

Residential Placement

- Provides intensive supervision and behavior management on a 24-hour-per-day basis for youth with severe conduct problems
- In addition to individual therapy, youth in residential settings often also receive family therapy and case management services

Medications for CD and ODD: Medication is not considered effective in treating CD or ODD. No medications have received approval from the Food and Drug Administration (FDA) for the treatment of CD or ODD. Some medications, however, are helpful for treating the impulsive aggressive behavior displayed by youth with CD or ODD (Tcheremissine, Cherek, & Lane, 2004). These medications are the following:

> *Risperidone (Risperdal®):* This medication, used to treat impulsive aggression in children, is usually well tolerated. Side effects include drowsiness, headaches, and weight gain.
>
> *Haloperidol (Haldol®) and Chlorpromazine (Thorazine®):* These medications can reduce severe aggression in children and are typically used in hospitals and other residential settings. Because of their serious side effects, they are usually not recommended for use with children and adolescents.

Youth with CD and ODD often have other mental health problems, such as attention-deficit/hyperactivity disorder, depression, bipolar disorder, and substance abuse. Medications used to treat these problems can sometimes help symptoms of CD and ODD.

Attention-Deficit/Hyperactivity Disorder

Defining Attention-Deficit/Hyperactivity Disorder: Attention-deficit/hyperactivity disorder (ADHD) is a behavioral disorder with three major symptoms: (1) inattention, (2) hyperactivity, and (3) impulsivity.

Signs of *inattention* include the following:

- Becoming easily distracted by sights and sounds ignored by others
- Failing to pay attention to details and making careless mistakes
- Rarely following instructions carefully and completely
- Losing or forgetting things like toys, pencils, books, and tools needed for a task

Signs of *hyperactivity* and *impulsivity* include the following:

- Feeling restless, often fidgeting with hands or feet or squirming
- Running, climbing, or leaving a seat in situations where sitting or quiet behavior is expected
- Blurting out answers before hearing the whole question
- Having difficulty waiting in line or for a turn

Diagnosing ADHD: Children with ADHD often display different patterns of behavior. The *DSM-IV-TR* identifies three subtypes of ADHD:

> *ADHD, Combined Type.* Children with this subtype display symptoms of inattention and hyperactivity-impulsivity.

ADHD, Predominantly Inattentive Type. Children with this subtype mainly have symptoms of inattention.

ADHD, Predominantly Hyperactive-Impulsive Type. This subtype is characterized mainly by symptoms of hyperactivity and impulsivity.

An accurate diagnosis is key to the successful treatment of ADHD. Not every child who is hyperactive, inattentive, or impulsive has an attention disorder. Many children sometimes blurt out things they did not mean to say, bounce from one task to another, or become confused and forgetful. How can mental health professionals tell if the problem is ADHD? In order to assess whether a child has ADHD, mental health professionals follow specific guidelines:

- The behaviors must appear before age 7.
- The behaviors must be present for at least 6 months.
- The behaviors must be more frequent or severe than in other children of the same age.
- The behaviors must lead to impairment in at least two areas of a child's life, such as school, home, or social settings.

Treatment of ADHD

Attention-deficit/hyperactivity disorder can be treated with medication and/or psychosocial interventions. Most mental health professionals recommend using a combination of medication and psychosocial interventions to help a child with ADHD.

Medications for ADHD: For decades, medications have been used to treat the symptoms of ADHD. Four medications in a class of drugs known as *stimulants* seem to be the most effective in both children and adults. These are the following:

- Methylphenidate (Ritalin® or Concerta®)
- Dextroamphetamine (Dexedrine® or DextroStat®)
- Adderall® (a combination of amphetamine-related medications)

Another medication is Strattera® (atomoxetine). Strattera has been recently approved by the FDA and is the first *nonstimulant* medication for ADHD. These medications are effective in reducing ADHD symptoms in 70% to 80% of children with the disorder (MTA Cooperative Group, 2004). In fact, research tells us that stimulant medications are the *most* effective way to treat the symptoms of ADHD (MTA Cooperative Group, 1999).

Despite the fact that stimulant medications work really well for children with ADHD, many parents have mixed feelings about whether to give their child medication. Some common questions parents have about stimulants include the following:

1. Are stimulant medications safe?

YES. Stimulants are some of the best-studied medications in use today. Results of many studies tell us that stimulants are safe and effective for the treatment of ADHD (Jensen, 2002).

2. Are stimulant medications addictive?

NO. Stimulants have some similarities, in terms of their chemical structure, to drugs of abuse like cocaine, but taking stimulants by mouth does not cause a child or adult to "get high." Taken orally, stimulants are unlikely to produce the type of effects that lead to substance abuse or addiction. Overall, the risk that a child will abuse or become addicted to stimulant medication is very low (Molina B., for the MTA Cooperative Group, 2007).

3. Do stimulant medications increase the chance of drug addiction later in life?

NO. Recent research suggests that stimulant medications may actually *protect* a child or adolescent against abusing drugs in adolescence or young adulthood (Molina B., for the MTA Cooperative Group, 2007).

In addition to addressing these questions, it is important to encourage parents to discuss medication concerns with their child's doctor.

Psychosocial Interventions for ADHD: Psychosocial interventions are an important part of treatment for a child with ADHD. These interventions include behavior therapy, social skills training, parent training, and educational interventions. Although these interventions are extremely valuable, they are often most helpful in combination with medication. Each of the psychosocial interventions for ADHD is described briefly next.

Behavior Therapy

- Teaches skills for monitoring and managing behavior
- Usually involves parents and teachers

Social Skills Training

- Through role playing and practice, teaches children how to interact effectively and appropriately with peers and adults

Parent Training

- Educates parents about ADHD
- Teaches parents strategies for managing their child's behavior

Educational Interventions

- Includes a variety of modifications and services that can assist a child with ADHD in school (see Part 3 of this book for more information)

In addition to these treatments, there are a variety of *alternative treatments* for ADHD. These include biofeedback, special diets, vitamin and herbal supplements, hypnosis, and meditation. It is important to know that alternative treatments have *not* been proven effective for the treatment of ADHD.

Posttraumatic Stress Disorder

Posttraumatic stress disorder (PTSD) is a trauma-related anxiety disorder commonly seen in children and adolescents in foster care. Exposure to violence, natural disasters, sexual or physical abuse, and removal from home are just a few examples of common traumatic events that can occur in the lives of children and adolescents. Children who have been exposed to traumatic events show a wide range of reactions, such as fear, loss of trust in adults, and avoidance. All children who experience a traumatic event need support from adults to avoid long-term emotional difficulties. Most will recover quite quickly, but a few will develop PTSD and require treatment.

Defining PTSD

According to the *DSM-IV-TR,* PTSD involves the development of a specific set of symptoms after exposure to a serious or life-threatening event. These symptoms are the following:

1. Reexperiencing of the traumatic event by frequent memories, dreams, feeling like the event is happening again, and physical or emotional distress when reminded of the event.
2. Avoidance of people, places, or thoughts related to the traumatic event.
3. Emotional numbing or hyperarousal. Loss of interest in previously fun activities and feelings of detachment are examples of emotional numbing. Increased alertness and irritability are examples of hyperarousal.

Diagnosing PTSD

Diagnosing PTSD in children requires skilled, direct, and sensitive interviewing of both the child and the parent. Given that distress is a normal reaction to a traumatic event, mental health professionals follow guidelines provided by the *DSM-IV-TR* in order to determine when the symptoms indicate PTSD as opposed to a normal reaction that will resolve in time. These guidelines are the following:

- The traumatic stressor must be of an extreme nature.
- The symptoms must start after the traumatic event.
- The symptoms must be present for at least one month.
- The symptoms must get in the way of the child's functioning at home, at school, and/or in the community.

Treatment of PTSD

Experts agree that children with PTSD should first be treated with a psychosocial intervention (Foa, Davidson & Frances, 1999). Sometimes, medication may also be necessary. Information about psychosocial interventions and medications for PTSD follows.

Psychosocial Interventions: *Trauma-focused cognitive behavioral therapy* is one PTSD psychosocial intervention with strong support. This intervention has several parts:

1. *Parental Involvement:* It is important that parents be included in the treatment (especially for young children) or seek their own treatment if necessary in order to more effectively help their children resolve PTSD symptoms.
2. *Psychoeducation:* Teaches the child and parent about trauma, PTSD, and how treatment can help.
3. *Anxiety Management:* Teaches the child techniques such as relaxation, thought stopping, and positive imagery to help the child gain a sense of control over thoughts and feelings.
4. *Exposure Therapy:* Involves gradual but direct discussion of the traumatic event in a safe, controlled environment. This allows processing of thoughts and feelings related to the trauma. In cases where children are not able to discuss the trauma, drawing, play, and other techniques might be helpful.
5. *Cognitive Restructuring:* Helps children identify and correct inaccurate thoughts or beliefs related to the trauma (e.g., "It was all my fault").

Medications for PTSD: No medications have been specifically approved by the FDA for the treatment of PTSD in children. Medication is prescribed for a child with PTSD when the child has not responded well to psychosocial interventions and/or has severe PTSD symptoms. Table 11.1 lists some of the

Table 11.1 **Medications for PTSD**

Medication	Target Symptoms
Selective serotonin reuptake inhibitors (SSRIs) (e.g., Prozac®, Zoloft®, Celexa®)	Sleep disturbance Irritability Hypervigilance Depression Panic
Adrenergic agents (e.g., Catapres®, Inderal®, Tenex®)	Hyperarousal Impulsivity
Mood stabilizers (e.g., Lithium, Depakote®, Tegretol®)	Lack of emotional control
Atypical neuroleptics (e.g., Risperdal®)	Severe self-harm behavior Psychosis Aggression Dissociation

medications typically prescribed for PTSD in children and the symptoms they address. Parents should discuss any concerns they have about medications prescribed to their child with their child's doctors.

Other Anxiety Disorders

In addition to PTSD, there are several other anxiety disorders that can affect children and adolescents. The brief descriptions of these disorders provided here are based on the *DSM-IV-TR.*

Separation Anxiety Disorder. This disorder is most common in children ages 7 to 9. Children with separation anxiety disorder experience extreme anxiety when away from home or separated from their parents. Children with this disorder may also avoid going places alone, have nightmares about separation, refuse to go to school, and demand that someone sleep with them at night.

Specific Phobias. Children and adolescents with a specific phobia have a strong fear of an object (e.g., snakes or insects) or a situation (e.g., elevators or planes) that presents little actual danger. The feared object or situation is avoided as much as possible and causes extreme anxiety when encountered.

Social Phobia. Social phobia is a strong fear of social or performance situations involving unfamiliar people or evaluation by others. Children and youth with social phobia try to avoid certain social situations. When faced with these situations, they experience intense physical symptoms of anxiety (e.g., pounding heart, sweating, feeling faint, and so on).

Generalized Anxiety Disorder. Children and adolescents with generalized anxiety disorder have excessive and uncontrollable worry about everyday things, such as academics, sports, performance, health, and so on. The worry is associated with restlessness, fatigue, difficulty concentrating, irritability, muscle tension, or sleep disturbance.

Panic Disorder. Children and adolescents with panic disorder have repeated, unexpected panic attacks. They also must have persistent anxiety about future attacks or the consequences of attacks. Panic attacks have both physical symptoms (e.g., racing heart, dizziness, shortness of breath, or trembling) and emotional symptoms (e.g., fear of losing control, going crazy, or dying). Children and adolescents with panic disorder may avoid situations that cause anxiety or panic.

Obsessive-Compulsive Disorder. Children and adolescents with obsessive-compulsive disorder have recurring bothersome thoughts (obsessions) and repetitive behaviors or rituals (compulsions). These obsessions and compulsions are time consuming and cause anxiety or distress. For example, an adolescent may wash his hands constantly (compulsion) because he fears contamination (obsession).

Diagnosing Anxiety Disorders

Anxiety disorders are one of the most common psychiatric disorders affecting youth, but youth with these disorders often never receive treatment. Left untreated, youth with anxiety disorders are at higher risk to perform poorly in school and to abuse drugs or alcohol. They also tend to have less developed social skills.

When diagnosing an anxiety disorder, mental health professionals consider the following:

- Is the focus of the anxiety typical compared to other children of the same age?
- How intense is the nature of the anxiety and worry?
- Does the anxiety significantly interfere with the child's school, social, or family functioning?
- Are the symptoms caused by a medical condition or substance use?

Treatment of Anxiety Disorders

Cognitive-behavioral therapy and certain medications have been proven to work best for the treatment of anxiety disorders. For some children, cognitive-behavioral therapy alone leads to significant improvement. For others, a combination of cognitive-behavioral therapy and medication is needed. Experts in the treatment of childhood anxiety advise against treating anxiety disorders *only* with medication (Practice Parameter for the Assessment and Treatment of Children and Adolescents with Anxiety Disorders, 2007).

Psychosocial Interventions: Cognitive-behavioral therapy is one psychosocial treatment for anxiety disorders that has been proven to work. Cognitive-behavioral therapy for anxiety disorders has components similar to cognitive-behavioral therapy for PTSD (see p. 118). These components include parental involvement, psychoeducation, anxiety management, exposure, and cognitive restructuring.

Medications for Anxiety Disorders: Table 11.2 lists the classes and specific types of medications that are used to treat anxiety disorders in children and adolescents. A few of these medications have been specifically approved by the FDA for the treatment of obsessive-compulsive disorder. The FDA has not approved any medications for the treatment of other anxiety disorders in children.

Table 11.2 *Medications for Anxiety Disorders*

Medication	Use
Selective serotonin reuptake inhibitors (SSRIs) (e.g., Luvox®, Prozac®, Zoloft®, Paxil®, Celexa®)	Luvox®, Prozac®, and Zoloft® are FDA approved for the treatment of obsessive-compulsive disorder. All of the listed SSRIs are used to treat anxiety disorders.
Tricyclic antidepressants (TCAs) (e.g., Anafranil®)	FDA approved for the treatment of obsessive-compulsive disorder but has more unpleasant side effects than SSRIs
Benzodiazepines	Provide short-term relief of anxiety symptoms

Depression

Defining Depression

Depression is a mood disorder that can affect both children and adolescents. Children and adolescents who have experienced abuse, neglect, and other negative life events are at risk for depression.

Some of the common symptoms of depression in children and adolescents are the following:

- Sad or irritable mood
- Loss of interest in fun activities
- Significant weight gain or loss
- Difficulty sleeping or sleeping all the time
- Feeling restless or very slowed down
- Significant fatigue/loss of energy
- Feelings of worthlessness
- Strong feelings of guilt
- Difficulty concentrating and/or making decisions
- Hopelessness about the future
- Recurrent thoughts of death and/or suicide

In addition to these symptoms, there are several "red flags" that may indicate depression. These include the following:

- Academic underachievement and school failure
- School attendance problems
- Increasing levels of family conflict
- Increasing use of illegal substances
- Physical symptoms (e.g., headaches, chronic fatigue, or stomach problems)

Diagnosing Depression

Depression can be difficult to diagnose in children and adolescents because the symptoms of the disorder can go unnoticed by parents and other adults. Diagnosing depression as early as possible is very important, however, because, when untreated, depression can lead to suicide. Asking children and adolescents about their feelings is one way parents can uncover symptoms of depression that may otherwise go unnoticed. Having some of the symptoms of depression does not necessarily mean that a child is depressed. When diagnosing depression, mental health professionals follow these guidelines (*DSM-IV-TR*):

- Five or more symptoms of depression must be present during a 2-week period.

- The symptoms must impair the child's functioning in school, with friends, or at home.
- The symptoms are not caused by a medical condition or the use of drugs or alcohol.
- The symptoms are not better explained by bereavement after the loss of a loved one.

Treatment of Depression

Both medication and psychosocial interventions can be used to treat depression in children and adolescents. Information about common medications and psychosocial interventions for depression follows.

Medications for Depression: *Selective serotonin reuptake inhibitors (SSRIs) and tricyclic antidepressants (TCAs)* are used for the treatment of depression in children and adolescents.

> *SSRIs:* An SSRI is usually the first type of medication prescribed to treat youth depression. Prozac®, Zoloft®, and Celexa® are examples of SSRIs used to treat depression. These medications take approximately 4 to 6 weeks to begin working. Although SSRIs are effective, the FDA has issued a warning about SSRIs because they may cause worsening of depressive symptoms and increased suicidal thoughts in some youth.
>
> *TCAs:* Although effective in the treatment of depression, TCAs are not used as often as SSRIs because they have more side effects. They may be indicated for the treatment of depression in youth who are also diagnosed with ADHD.

Although medications work well for children with depression, many parents have mixed feelings about them. It is important to encourage parents to discuss any concerns they may have about medication with their child's doctor.

Psychosocial Interventions for Depression: Two types of psychosocial interventions—cognitive-behavioral therapy and interpersonal psychotherapy for depressed adolescents—have been found helpful in the treatment of youth depression.

Cognitive-behavioral therapy for depression has several important components:

- *Psychoeducation:* Teaches children and parents about the nature of depression and the relationship between thinking, behavior, and mood

- *Behavioral activation:* Helps children and adolescents to increase their daily activity level and participate in more pleasurable activities
- *Cognitive restructuring:* Teaches children and adolescents to change their thinking patterns and increase positive thinking

Interpersonal psychotherapy for depressed adolescents provides education to adolescents about the nature and causes of depression and focuses on helping adolescents improve their relationships with others as a way of decreasing their depression.

Bipolar Disorder

Defining Bipolar Disorder

Bipolar disorder, also known as *manic-depressive illness,* is a type of mood disorder. The symptoms of bipolar disorder may at first be mistaken for the normal ups and downs of childhood or adolescence. However, the mood swings associated with bipolar disorder last for months or years and are highly impairing for the child and the family.

Bipolar disorder can begin with either manic or depressive symptoms. According to the *DSM-IV-TR,* bipolar disorder involves repeated episodes of mania, depression, and/or mixed manic/depressive symptom states. These episodes involve extreme shifts in mood, energy, and behavior that interfere with the child's daily functioning.

Mania involves an *elated* (overly silly, goofy, or excitable) or extremely irritable mood. Common symptoms of mania are the following:

- Exaggerated sense of one's own importance or ability
- Racing thoughts
- Pressured speech
- Decreased need for sleep
- Increased goal-directed activity or hyperactivity
- Distractibility
- Excessive reckless or risk taking behaviors, with disregard for consequences (e.g., "fly" off roofs; increased sexual thoughts, feelings, or behavior; or use of explicit sexual language)

The symptoms must be severe enough to cause marked impairment in functioning or require hospitalization to prevent harm to self or others, or psychotic features are present. Examples of psychotic features are hallucinations (i.e., seeing or hearing things that are not there), paranoia (thinking that people are out to get them), and bizarre thoughts.

Depression involves *sad or irritable mood* (or, in children, mood may be explosive) or a persistent *loss of interest in previously enjoyed activities.* Common symptoms include the following:

- Significant change in appetite or weight (or failure to gain weight in children)
- Sleep disturbance
- Loss of energy or fatigue
- Physical slowing or agitation
- Feelings of inappropriate guilt or worthlessness
- Difficulties in concentration
- Recurrent thoughts of death or suicide

Diagnosis of Bipolar Disorder

Bipolar disorder in children is one of the most difficult disorders to diagnose. Effective treatment depends on an accurate diagnosis of bipolar disorder. An accurate diagnosis of bipolar disorder requires careful observation over an extended period of time. It takes into account developmental differences that might influence the expression of bipolar symptoms.

Professionals consider the following guidelines in diagnosing a child with bipolar disorder:

- Is there a presence of persistent mania specific symptoms?
- What is the course of the symptoms, patterns of the episodes, and response to treatment?
- Do the symptoms significantly interfere with the child's functioning at school, at home, or in the community?
- Are there other things that might be causing these symptoms (e.g., other mental disorders, substance use, metabolic conditions, neurological disorders, or other medical conditions)?
- Is there a family history of mood disorders or bipolar disorder?

Children who have bipolar disorder very often have a co-occurring mental disorder (e.g., ADHD, oppositional defiant disorder, or conduct disorder). A profile of the child's associated mental disorders is critical to treatment success. Treatment for symptoms of the other disorder(s) may set off or worsen manic symptoms. Further, these youngsters are at high risk for substance-related disorders and suicide.

Treatment of Bipolar Disorder

To date, treatment of bipolar disorder in children and adolescents is based primarily on scientific evidence and clinical experience with adults (Practice Parameter for the Assessment and Treatment of Children and Adolescents with Bipolar Disorder, 2007). Medications are considered a first-line treatment for bipolar disorder, with psychosocial treatments as an add-on. Because of the episodic or cyclical nature of bipolar disorder, symptoms change over the course of the illness. The child should be reassessed over time to ensure appropriate treatment for the different phases of the disorder. The child and family should be thoroughly educated about the signs and symptoms of bipolar disorder. Monitoring is necessary for timely change of treatment or restarting treatment in order to prevent relapse. It is important to encourage parents to work closely with their child's physician in discussing treatment options and making decisions about any changes in medication.

Youngsters who are in the midst of a severe episode may need to be hospitalized for their own safety or for the safety of others. Depending on the severity of their illness, regular school attendance may not be possible for some youngsters, and specialized programs may be necessary. Youngsters with bipolar disorder often have complicated clinical needs that require the integration of several services. These services may include medication management, psychosocial interventions, special education or vocational services, and case management. Out-of-home placement may be also necessary for youngsters who cannot be safely maintained in their own homes.

If left untreated, bipolar disorder in children and adolescents is associated with many negative outcomes over time, including being less responsive to treatment, legal involvement, multiple hospitalizations, substance use, and suicide.

Pharmacologic Treatments: To date, pharmacologic treatments in children with bipolar disorder are based on limited data (Practice Parameter for the Assessment and Treatment of Children and Adolescents with Bipolar Disorder, 2007). These data provide preliminary support for the use the following drugs as first-line treatment in children and adolescents:

> *Mood stabilizers:* Used to reduce the number and severity of manic symptoms and prevent recurrence of manic and depressive episodes. These include lithium and valproate (Depakote®). Carbamazepine (Tegretol®) has received sparse support for mania symptoms in children.
> *Atypical antipsychotics:* Useful for controlling mania symptoms, especially in children presenting with continuous, rapid cycling, and mixed symptom states. These medications include risperidone (Risperdal®), quetiapine (Seroquel®), olanzapine (Zyprexa®), ziprasidone (Geodon®).

Other anticonvulsant drugs, such as gabapentin (Neurontin®) and lamotrigine (Lamictal®), may be prescribed to children who have not responded to other medications. On occasion, electroconvulsive therapy may be used to treat bipolar disorder in adolescents, generally in those who cannot tolerate or have not responded to other medications.

Medication Caution for Bipolar Disorder

Antidepressants: The use of antidepressant medication without a mood stabilizer to treat individuals with depression may bring about symptoms of mania in those who have bipolar disorder.

Stimulants: The use of stimulant medications to treat ADHD or ADHD-like symptoms in a child with bipolar disorder may worsen manic symptoms.

Because of the high rates of co-occurrence with other disorders and the complicated nature of bipolar disorder in children, the use of multiple medications (polypharmacy) is quite common.

Side Effects of Mood Stabilizers and Atypical Antipsychotics: The use of mood stabilizers can be associated with potentially serious side effects. Before starting medication for bipolar disorder for their child, parents should ask their physician about possible side effects and their likelihood of occurrence. Children who are taking these medications should be carefully monitored by a physician. Parents should be encouraged to discuss medication concerns with their child's doctor.

Psychosocial Treatments: Psychosocial interventions for bipolar disorders are directed at managing risks. These are factors that may influence the course and the severity of impairment associated with the bipolar symptoms. In adults with bipolar disorder, psychoeducation and cognitive treatments have been associated with lowered relapse rates when combined with medication treatment. The key elements of these treatments are described next.

Family Psychoeducation (Individually or Group Based)

- Educates the child and family about the disorder and common co-occurring disorders
- Educates about the role of medications, other mental health interventions, and school interventions
- Provides opportunities for families to address the impact of managing the child's symptoms on the family
- Teaches the family ways to communicate more effectively to minimize negative expressed emotions (e.g., criticism) that are associated with relapse and slower recovery
- Teaches family positive behavior management techniques and ways to provide structure and routine, including minimizing sleep disruption
- Often involves helping parents work with the school system to educate teachers about the disorder

Monitoring Mood

- Teaches child and family to monitor the child's moods to identify emotional cycles and specific events that set them off

Affect Regulation/Anger Management

- Teaches family members strategies to deal with mood swings and explosive outbursts

- Teaches the child anger management techniques to deal with his or her irritable and explosive moods
- Teaches strategies to manage stress and problem solve, including scheduling pleasant activities to improve mood

Cognitive Restructuring

- Teaches the child to identify and understand feelings and how they may be related to thoughts and behaviors
- Teaches the child and family to reframe behaviors associated with the disorder to avoid the cycle of negative thoughts and feelings that leads to a negative sense of self, an aspect of depression
- Teaches ways to deal with unrealistic thought processes that are part of the disorder
- Teaches child/family to focus on helpful and positive thoughts

Relapse Prevention

- Helps the family and child strengthen and generalize skills learned in treatment to maintain gains outside of treatment
- Helps the family and child identify shifts in moods and behavior that may indicate a need to restart treatment or seek additional help

Building a Support Network

- Helps the family and child identify individuals who can help support them through difficult situations
- Identifies appropriate community supports that the family can access

Substance Abuse

It is fairly common for children and adolescents to experiment with drugs or alcohol. For some youth, experimentation is temporary and does not lead to substance abuse. For others, experimentation leads to increased use and abuse of drugs and alcohol.

Defining Substance Abuse

The main characteristic of substance abuse is repeated use of drugs or alcohol that interferes with an individual's ability to fulfill his or her responsibilities. Youth who abuse alcohol or drugs continue to use these substances even when doing so leads to negative consequences.

Diagnosing Substance Abuse

In order to be diagnosed with substance abuse, an individual must show one or more of the patterns of substance use that cause significant problems or distress during at least a 12-month period. These patterns are as follows:

- Repeated substance use leading to failure to fulfill responsibilities at work, school, or home
- Repeated substance use in situations in which it is physically dangerous
- Repeated substance-related legal problems
- Continued substance use despite having repeated social or interpersonal problems caused or exacerbated by the effects of the substance

Causes of Substance Abuse

The exact cause of youth substance abuse is difficult to identify. Genetic, social, and environmental factors all likely contribute to the development of substance abuse in youth. There are several risk factors associated with youth substance abuse. These risk factors include the following:

- Family history of substance abuse
- Depression
- Low self-esteem
- Feelings of isolation or not fitting in

Treatment of Substance Abuse

There are a many different treatment options for youth suffering from substance abuse. These options differ in terms of their location, intensity, length, and scope (Williams and Chang, 2000). Generally, treatment falls into four categories. These categories are described next.

Short Hospital Inpatient Programs: These programs typically last 4 to 6 weeks and offer a range of services to adolescents with substance abuse problems. Services usually include individual counseling, group therapy, family therapy, medication for other psychological problems, schooling, and recreational activities. Many hospital inpatient programs for substance abuse also have an Alcoholics Anonymous component for youth.

Outpatient Programs: The focus of outpatient substance abuse programs is usually on individual counseling, but sometimes family therapy is included. Youth in outpatient substance abuse programs typically attend one or two sessions a week. The length of these programs varies from several weeks to 6 months or more.

Residential or Day Treatment Programs: These programs usually last from 6 months to a year. They provide a highly structured therapeutic community where youth can address their substance abuse issues and receive other services.

Life Skills Training Programs: These programs provide an intensive 3- to 4-week outdoor experience to youth with substance abuse problems. The goal is to expose youth to a drug-free lifestyle and opportunities to experience personal growth. The hope is that this experience will help youth resist substance abuse in the future.

Assessing Treatment

There has not been enough research to clearly show what type of substance treatment is the best for a given adolescent. However, there is some evidence that outpatient family therapy for substance abuse is more effective than other forms of outpatient substance abuse treatments (Practice Parameter for the Assessment and Treatment of Children and Adolescents with Substance Use Disorders, 2007). It is important for parents seeking substance abuse treatment for their children to find out as much as they can about a given program before enrolling their child in a program.

Self-Study

After reviewing this chapter, ask yourself the following questions:

1. What is my role with parents regarding a child's diagnosis and treatment?

2. What specific disorders should I be familiar with in my work as a parent advisor?

3. How can I find out more about specific disorders?

Part III

Meeting Children's Needs
Within the School System

RueZalia Watkins

James Rodriguez

Lisa Hunter Romanelli

Polly Gipson

Making Home and School Partnerships Work

S chools play an essential role in the lives of all children. In some areas of the country, schools provide several levels of support for today's busy, working families. There are school communities that have health services and/ or mental health services right inside the school. There are also schools that house social service or juvenile justice offices as well. Whether or not the families you work with have comprehensive schools such as these, a school is still a community in itself with many great resources for families.

This chapter focuses on how parents can work with the school system—and with teachers in particular—to benefit their child's education. As a parent advisor, you can help parents form effective partnerships with their child's teachers.

School Resources

It is important to help parents know the ins and outs of school and education structures. They will need to effectively navigate the school system to ensure that their children's academic and social needs are met. Parents need to know who does what and where to go for help. When meeting with families about school issues, try asking parents the following questions:

- "How is your relationship with your child's teacher?"
- "Who do you communicate with in the school besides your child's teacher?"
- "How did you meet the teacher or establish this relationship?"
- "Are you involved in any activities within the school community?"

Activity/Personnel	Everyday	Days
Gifted education		
Bilingual Education		
Accelerated programs		
Multiple lunch periods		
Alternative physical education		
Art/music instruction		
After School Programs		
Driving classes		
Health services		
Mental health services		
Guidance counselors		
Deans/advisors		
Social workers		
School psychologist		
Child planning team		
Special education services		
Special education classes		
SES/tutoring		

Activity/Personnel	Everyday	Days
General equivalency diploma		
Adult education		
Parent programs		
No Child Left Behind schoolwide projects		
Parent Teacher Association / Parent Teacher Organization / Parent Association / Parent Organization		
County offices		
Juvenile justice		
Family court		
In-house suspension		
Section 504 coordinator		

- "What types of things do the parents or PTA do in the school?"
- "Are there any extra programs or services in your child's school?"
- "Have you ever gone to your local district, county, or regional education office for assistance?"

Questions like these will allow you to learn how much a family knows about the school system and to what extent they are involved in it.

You may want to go over "Who and What Is in Your Child's School?" with families. Most schools will have a few things on this list. The idea is to validate parents' existing knowledge while exposing them to possible resources and future ideas for their own advocacy in their child's school.

The U.S. Department of Education has staff responsible for educational policy, practice, implementation, and research (see Appendix A). Your state department of education has staff responsible for everything from curriculum to lunch to transportation. Local education offices have a lot of information and services for students and their families. You should gather materials and resources from these local, county, district, city, and/or regional education offices to provide to families. Parents can contact these offices to get the information necessary to help solve their educational issue or dilemma, with or without your assistance. See Chapter 16 for more information on the process for accessing services and Chapter 13 for a list of services available in a general education setting.

Once parents experience the fulfillment stemming from their own success in getting their child's needs met, they may also want to advocate for future resources for their child's school. Looking at this list of possible programs in a school may encourage parents to ask why they do not have a particular service in their school. They can use the information that they received from you to contact the appropriate education office, ask questions, and seek resources for their entire school community. In this way, parents are empowered to advocate for school improvements for their own child and other children and families as well.

Helping Parents Partner With a Child's Teacher

Before parents dive into seeking services, it is crucial that they have established a relationship with their child's teachers. Whether or not a family's child needs special services and accommodations, the best place for a parent to begin is with the child's teacher. In general, encourage parents to work first with their child's teacher and involve others only as needed. In some circumstances, however, it may be necessary to have others involved immediately.

Teachers and parents share the responsibility for a child's education as partners. Teachers need to recognize what a powerful asset parents are. Parents need to appreciate what a powerful role teachers play in a child's success. Parents and teachers must work together effectively to ensure the child's achievement of academic and behavioral goals.

A good teacher can make a tremendous difference in the life of a child with distinct needs. Effective teachers use a mix of patience, structure, consistency, positive discipline, and nurturance. They know how to pair children, group children, and keep them actively engaged in learning. They may use a variety of multisensory teaching techniques to get consistent responses from students during instruction.

Establishing a Teacher–Parent Partnership

Parents can expect and receive cooperation from most teachers by sharing information with the teacher about what their child needs and responds well to. To establish a good working relationship with teachers, it helps if parents acknowledge teachers' expertise, rely on their input and feedback, and recognize the difficulties that are inherent in their job. Working with a child with mental illness can place a burden on teachers. Teachers are often unaware of the different types of mental illnesses that affect children. They may have received little direction or training on how to effectively manage mental health issues and behaviors in the classroom setting. This can leave the teacher with few options for preventing or addressing concerns as they arise. Parents may be able to offer teachers invaluable support by sharing information on mental illness and the many strategies that may help a child in a classroom. Parental involvement may make a real impact on the efforts teachers make with children.

Very often, things can go wrong in schools and lead to frustrating situations. Regardless of the situation at hand, parents need to approach teachers and school personnel in an open, nondefensive, yet assertive way. In your work as a parent advisor, emphasize that despite obstacles, parents and teachers can become true collaborators. Positive changes in student achievement, attitude, and behavior can occur when teachers and parents partner in promoting the learning and success of the child.

In every interaction with a child's teacher, parents have the opportunity to build an effective partnership. The following handout contains some tips to give parents in order to make that partnership work.

Partnering With Teachers: Tips for Parents

- Arrange to take the child to school during the first week of classes and introduce yourself to the teacher.

- Ask the teacher how you can reach him or her and what the best number and time of day is to call.

- Establish positive, frequent communication.

- If you have a child with mental illness or behavior problem, you should call the teacher and touch base *before* there is a "problem."

- Talk to the teacher at the first sign of a problem—do not wait!

- Request a copy of your child's schedule so that you can discuss the day with your child more effectively.

- Consider using a daily school–home notebook to communicate success, concerns, or skills for the child to work on.

- Take every opportunity to show you appreciate the teacher. For example, praise your child's teacher in front of your child.

- Keep the teacher informed of any important changes in your child's life or treatment.

- Coordinate a behavior management program with the teacher so everyone is working on the same thing.

- Make school behavior and academic success part of your child's reward program at home.

- Ask the teacher about outside services or additional activities that can supplement a specific course being covered in the class.

- Ask if there is a pattern to the assignments so that you can help your child organize (e.g., current events homework is often over the weekend). Ask about the homework policy (e.g., who is supposed to correct it).

Meeting and partnering can be a time-consuming and often difficult task. You should assist parents in planning how they are going to maintain school contact and address these various strategies for partnering.

Suggestions for School Accommodations

Although a teacher may be willing to partner with the parent, he or she may not be familiar with the techniques that work best for children with mental illness. Remind parents that these techniques are only suggestions, not demands that parents can place on the teacher. Furthermore, each teacher's style and reaction may be different. In addition, parents need to keep in mind that not all techniques will work with every child. Parents should establish a working relationship with the teacher to find appropriate modifications and accommodations to help maximize their child's potential and productivity.

When the Partnership Is Not Working

Sometimes parents may find it difficult to establish a good partnership with their child's teacher. In the event of a difficult relationship, it is important that parents continue working toward an effective relationship for the benefit of their child. The following handout contains some tips to help families work with their child's teacher even when things are difficult between them.

If these tactics do not work, parents should talk to their school administrator. First, however, they should consider whether the current school setting is able to meet their child's needs or whether their child needs a higher level of service (see Chapter 14).

Tips for Parent Advisors

At times, parents may ask you to meet their child's teacher with them. Here are some tips for acting as a parent advisor with the child's teacher:

- Practice explaining the child's diagnosis to the teacher (you may want to use language learned from this guide).
- Practice suggesting specific tips the teacher could use in the classroom that may work well with the child. Remember that these tips should not be communicated as demands or expectations placed on the teacher. Instead, these should be offered as helpful suggestions that will make the classroom environment better for the child and the teacher's job easier.

- Choose one or two issues to deal with at a time

- Address the teacher directly with concerns

- Stick to the original issue without adding a new one until the first concerns are solved

- Provide the teacher and school with information on your child's disability

- Take a parent advisor to school meetings

- Enlist your child's guidance counselor to facilitate communication

- Know what your child needs for the educational situation to improve

- Consider having your child moved to another classroom

- Know your child's special education rights and your parental rights

- Work together with the teacher through open dialogue to identify what may or may not work best for the child in the classroom. Discuss any modifications needed to the techniques deemed appropriate. Illustrate these changes by writing them down on paper. It is also helpful to come up with examples of when problems may occur and address how to work through them.
- Encourage parents to ask the teacher if there is anything they can do to assist the teacher or the class as a whole.

Self-Study

After reviewing this chapter, ask yourself the following questions:

1. What are some resources available in the school systems of families I work with?

2. Where are the local school district offices, county education office, and state education offices located?

3. How can families in my area advocate for resources in their school?

4. What are some tips I can give parents to help them work with their child's teacher?

5. What are some things parents can do if they are having problems with a teacher?

6. How can I be of assistance when meeting teachers with parents?

School-Based Options
for Special Education

RueZalia Watkins

Lisa Hunter Romanelli

One of your greatest accomplishments as a parent advisor will be help-ing families get special education services without putting a child into a special education program. Many parents are surprised to learn that their child can get special education services while in a regular, general education classroom. Despite many advances in special education programs, many fami-lies still consider "special education" to be anything but special. This chapter outlines the broad array of services that are available to students in a general education setting. The two main types of supports are *supplementary aids and services* and *related services*. There are also several additional services that may be available to families.

The federal Individuals with Disabilities Education Improvement Act (IDEIA) requires that school districts provide free and appropriate special education services to students in a general education setting. General education settings are also called the least restrictive environment for students requiring special education services. Under IDEIA, an Individual Education Plan (IEP) must be created to detail both a child's need for services based on evaluations and the specific plan to implement them. Alternatively, services can be accessed through a Section 504 plan and renewed every year provided that a medical doctor details the services and reason they are needed. For more information on how to create an IEP or a Section 504 plan, see Chapter 16.

Supplementary Aids and Services

According to the federal definition in the IDEIA guidelines, supplementary aids and services "means aids, services and other supports that are provided in regular education classes, other education related settings and in extracurricular and nonacademic settings to enable children with disabilities to be educated with non-disabled children to the maximum extent possible in accordance with federal laws on least restrictive environments." Supplementary aids and services are a broad group that includes supports a family can get without an IEP, with an IEP, through a Section 504 plan, or through an intervention plan (see emergency services on p. 151).

Supplementary aids and services may include the following:

Instructional Adaptations: Change in the pacing or sequencing used to present information.

Instructional Practices: Cross-age tutoring, peer partnerships, and group projects.

Curriculum Accommodations: Use of audiotapes, calculators, and word processors as well as changes in presentation mode (e.g., use of picture symbols or overheads with key points).

Individual Supports: Rephrasing questions and instructions, allowance for additional time to transition to other classes, main idea summaries, highlighted reading materials, and organizational aids.

Behavior Intervention Plans: These are detailed plans based on clear descriptions of the behaviors and knowledge of the triggers of the behaviors. They include specific instructional strategies to prevent the behaviors or to help the students deal with the results and consequences of the behaviors.

Resource Room Services: These may be called different names in different locations around the country but are services provided by special education teachers to help students with reading or math. They are given either individually or in small groups.

Collaborative Team Teaching: This is an integrated form of instruction provided by a special education teacher and a general education teacher in one classroom filled with mostly general education students and a few students with disabilities.

Test Accommodations: This category covers a broad array of procedures and formats to provide opportunities for students with special needs to demonstrate their knowledge and skills on standardized tests. It includes separate location, extended time, directions read and reread, answers recorded by any means necessary, use of calculators, use of markers, and other accommodations, depending on the recommendations detailed in the student's evaluations.

Alternative Assessments: These are procedures to modify a performance goal on a standardized test or to use a specially created test. Alternative assessments are designed to demonstrate the achievement of students with developmental delays.

Paraprofessional Supports: One-on-one support given to students for different reasons depending on your state. Usually these services are offered to prevent crisis, to help a student who is awaiting another placement, or to help a student traveling on the school bus.

With all these supplementary aids and services, it is important to help families determine if these services are needed for a short time or indefinitely. If they are needed indefinitely or perhaps more than a year, it is best to get evaluations and to go through the IEP process. It is also best to go through the IEP process to solidify the student's legal entitlement to the following services: test accommodations, resource room, collaborative teaching, alternative assessment, paraprofessional supports, and behavior intervention plans. Even though these services can be supported through Section 504 and other processes incorporated in intervention and prevention policies within a school, often only the IEP can ensure certain services and accommodations for students. This is because federal funding is available to support the services detailed on an IEP, whether the child is in a general education setting or any other kind of program.

Related Services

Related services are divided into two groups—general services and individual services. According to IDEIA federal guidelines, related services include transportation and developmental, corrective, and other supportive services required to assist a child with a disability to achieve in all aspects of education programs.

In a nutshell, *general* related services are services needed for groups of students in a class or school. These services are available to any student within a general education setting. This includes all services needed for evaluation and services given after evaluation, such as tutoring given to a group of students to help them improve academically.

Individual related services are exactly that: services needed by an individual student based on the evaluations and IEP team decisions. These are the one-on-one and small-group services that we usually seek to get on the IEP. Individual related services are usually "related" to the student's identified disability or classification.

The following list may not apply to every child, but the more you know about services, the more you will be able to help families. Some families may have children that require services across several systems. Other families may have children with two or more disorders. For example, a family might seek your help with their child who has attention-deficit/hyperactivity disorder *and* significant hearing loss. Or a family may need services for a child with a physical impairment who is also being treated for depression.

All the services listed here can be given in a general education setting provided that the evaluations document that the child is a student with a disability and has a need for these services to ensure academic progress with his or her nondisabled peers.

Audiology: This includes a broad array of services, including identification, auditory training, speech reading, counseling and guidance for families, and more. Services are usually provided by licensed professionals.

Counseling: This includes services provided by qualified social workers, psychologists, or guidance counselors to help students with school-related experiences. Examples are counseling to help a student who is unable to socialize with other students in the class or counseling to help a student learn to curb disruptive behavior in class. Note therapy and counseling are different. Therapy is highly individualized and deals with one's total life. School-based counseling involves helping the student learn and function in the school environment.

Early Identification and Assessment: This involves the implementation of a formal plan for identifying a disability as soon as possible in a child's life. For example, this includes early intervention programs for preschool children who may need to be evaluated and receive specialized services designed for young children.

Interpreting Services: These include services in cued language, sign language, and transcription; services for deaf and hearing-impaired students; and special interpreting services for students who are both deaf and blind.

Medical Services: These are services provided by a licensed physician to determine a child's medically related disability that results in the child's need for special education and related services. For example, psychiatric services can be provided by the school system to identify a student's mental or attention disorder and its impact on instruction and school life. These services are used to make specific recommendations about treatment for the identified illness.

Occupational Therapy: These are services provided by a qualified occupational therapist to improve, prevent, develop, or restore functions that are impaired or lost through illness, injury, or deprivation. The aim of therapy is that students can perform tasks completely and independently. For example, occupational therapy can help students with fine motor skills, such as handwriting or using scissors. In some areas, occupational therapists have helped students with activities designed to promote organization.

Orientation and Mobility: These are services provided to blind and visually impaired students to enable those students to attain safe movement within their environments.

Parent Counseling and Training: These are services designed to help parents in understanding the special needs of their child. Although provided for by federal law, their availability is often unknown to families and limited to families of young children or families whose children have certain classifications, such as autism or multiply disabled.

Physical Therapy: These are services provided by a qualified physical therapist to help students with the physical demands of navigating and functioning in the school environment.

Psychological Services: These services include evaluations, gathering and incorporating information about a student, consulting with staff in planning, providing counseling to students, and assisting in developing behavior intervention plans, strategies, and their implementation. For example, school psychologists can create specific activities to be included in a behavior intervention plan and help the appropriate staff perform these tasks.

Recreation: This includes assessment of leisure function, therapeutic recreation, leisure education, and recreation programs in the school.

Rehabilitation Counseling: This is provided by qualified personnel in individual or group sessions that focus on career development, employment preparation, achieving independence, and integration into the workplace as well as vocational rehabilitation.

School Health and Nurse Services: Health services may be provided by a qualified person or a nurse. Nurse services must be provided by a school nurse. For example, these services can help provide a free and appropriate public education as described on the child's IEP by providing the dispensing of medication.

Social Worker Services: These services include preparing a social or developmental history, group and individual counseling, helping families and students with adjustment issues or other problems, mobilizing resources, and assisting in the development of behavior intervention strategies. For example, to initiate the special education process, a social worker may meet with a family to gather information about the student's strengths, interests, weaknesses, development, and other relevant history.

Speech and Language Services: These include identification, diagnosis, and provision of speech and language services. These services are for the resolution or prevention of communication impairment that interfere with memory, reading, expressing language, and/or processing language. For example, speech and language services can help a student who has difficulty processing the language he or she hears and reads. Or they can help a student remember ideas and express these ideas in writing tasks.

Transportation: This includes travel to and from school and between schools as well as in and around the school building. It also includes travel training to accomplish all this. For example, travel training can be used to help students with impulse or attention disorders successfully transition from class to class. Travel training can also help a student with an anxiety disorder safely leave home and travel to school.

It is important to remember that the need for all these services must be documented in the evaluations, requested in IEP meetings, and detailed on all IEP documents. This includes transportation, especially given the ever-rising costs of gasoline. See Chapter 16 for specifics of what needs to be included on an IEP.

Other Helpful Services in a General Education Setting

The following are additional services that may be helpful to families whose children are in a general education setting.

Assistive Technology Services: These directly assist a child with a disability in the selection, acquisition, and/or use of a device or equipment used to increase, maintain, or improve the child's functional capacities. In some parts of the country, this may include everything from FM units for hearing to high-tech communication boards for students with no ability to form or vocalize words and speech patterns.

Extended School Year Services: These are special education and related services extended past the regular school year. These services include summer school to help students who need extra help and time to make progress and meet academic standards.

Nonacademic Services: These are supplementary aids and services designed to afford students with disabilities an equal opportunity to participate in nonacademic and extracurricular activities. Specific services are those determined appropriate and necessary by the child's IEP team. Activities and services include counseling, athletics, transportation, health services, recreational activities, special interest groups and clubs, and referrals to other agencies and employment.

Emergency or Intervention Services: For the most part, around the country, there are not any education emergency programs, offices, or services as such. Families, however, may feel like it is an emergency when they move and need a new school or when their child's behavior is escalating to the point of numerous phone calls to them during the workday. Educational emergencies for families are situations facing students that require immediate attention. When students face a crisis in the school, there are "emergency actions" that can be taken to help the child regardless of the reason or source of the need. A team consisting of the principal or the principal's designee, a guidance counselor, a teacher, the family, and the parent advisor can all meet to create an intervention plan. The child's therapist or psychiatrist can even join the meeting by phone or submit documentation to help with the intervention plan. This plan may include some of the supplementary aids and services discussed previously. It details which services can be used temporarily to support the child. For example, it may be used while the child adjusts to a new school. Or it may be used to prevent excessive behavior issues if the child is going through a difficult period. It may even be used pending future evaluations to develop an IEP. An intervention plan is a short-term solution and may not include some services, such as test accommodations.

Self-Study

After reviewing this chapter, ask yourself the following questions:

1. What is the "least restrictive environment" in regard to special education?

2. What is the difference between supplementary aids and services and related services?

3. What are some of the supports covered under supplementary aids and services?

4. What are some of the types of related services?

5. What are some of the other helpful services available in my area?

6. What processes can be used to access services?

7. What are considered emergency services within the school system?

Other Options for
Special Education

RueZalia Watkins

As the needs of students become more pronounced, services in a general education setting may not be enough. It may be necessary for parents to place their child in a more restrictive environment than the regular classroom. Options include special education programs, home instructions, day treatment or therapeutic schools, hospital-based instruction, and residential programs.

Special Education Programs

A child may be placed in a special education program to foster the child's improvement in behavior, attention, and learning in ways that lead to significant improvement in scholastic achievement. Parents may wish to consider special education programs if the child is nearing a transition to middle or high school in order to get as much help as possible before that transition year. Parents may also decide on a special education program if all the services delivered at different times by different providers are confusing or distracting for their child.

Special education programs are considered "restrictive environments" because they are not the "least restrictive environment." That is, they are not part of the general education classroom; they may be in a different classroom in the same school or a different school in the community. However, students in a special education program are supposed to meet the same academic standards and levels of achievements as the students in general education. They are expected to graduate with high school diplomas and reach other levels of achievement to the greatest extent possible. The reason for restrictive, special education programs is to make sure that students with disabilities get the intensive services they need to achieve academically and scholastically like their nondisabled peers. In your work with families, it is very important to help them remember that their children can learn, achieve, and grow into productive and successful adults. The purpose of education and specifically special education is to prepare students for future possibilities in their adult lives.

To access special education programs, an Individual Education Plan (IEP) must be generated. Note that Section 504 provides only services and/or accommodations, not access to a special program. It is also important to note that students can be placed in special education classrooms or programs part time. If a student excels in a certain subject area but has significant deficits in another, parents should be encouraged to request a special education program part time to address only the areas of weakness.

The following listing of special education programs are generally available in many schools within the public school system. Additional services and programs may be available in non–public school settings, but all special education programs must meet state guidelines. Check with your state department of education to determine what options are available in your area.

Student-to-Teacher Ratios

Special education programs may have different student-to-teacher ratios. Typical configurations are described as follows.

15:1 Special Education Programs (With or Without Related Services): These are usually in a high school setting with 15 students and one teacher. If related services are added, they should address a certain subject or content area. (See the later section regarding related services within special education programs.)

12:1 Special Education Programs (With or Without Related Services): These are usually in an elementary or middle school setting. Some schools have 12:1:1 with the additional adult being a paraprofessional or, even better, an assistant teacher; 12:1:1 or 15:1:1 class programs generally happen only in specialized private school programs.

6:1 Special Education Programs (With or Without Related Services): These are usually an extremely restricted environment for children with a variety of complex types of disabling conditions. Many of the children may have multiple conditions to be addressed, including physical, mental, developmental, and learning problems.

3:1 Special Education Programs (With or Without Related Services): These are usually early intervention or early childhood programs. Related services, such as counseling and/or speech and language services, can be provided in these programs for very young students.

Related services can be provided within all these special education programs. (See Chapter 13 for a list of related services.) It is crucial to help families secure these related services in special education programs. These services can ensure that children make adequate progress while in the program. It is also important not to forget essential services, such as transportation and testing accommodations. As is the case with all services, the need must be documented by the evaluations and included on the student's IEP.

Other Restrictive Educational Placements

Depending on a family's situation, a child's needs might not be best met by a special education program regardless of whether it is public or private or in the community or a neighboring county. Alternatives for parents to consider include the following.

Home Instruction

Home Instruction—Type I (With or Without Related Services): These are instructional services provided temporarily in the home for a few hours a day with a licensed teacher. Although these services are often successful, they take a toll on the child and family, particularly the child who gives up significant learning opportunities in social interaction, large-scale organization, transitioning from class to class, and learning throughout the school day. Specialists may be involved if related services are required on the IEP, which may give families more hours of services; however, a few hours of intense home instruction should be used only as a very temporary measure.

Home Instruction—Type II (With or Without Related Services): In most places around the country, this is called *homeschooling*. In this case, parents are the teachers. Instruction is based on an approved state and/or local (city) curriculum. Parents are given support through the home instruction office once their instructional plan has been approved. If their child needs related services, they will have to take them to a designated school.

Day Treatment or Therapeutic Schools

These are school programs that are usually dually licensed by the mental health and education systems of your state. An IEP is required to get into these programs. However, the goals and standards may be changed to help the child improve his or her mental health stability and academic/social functioning at the same time. Many of these programs may include case management, psychiatric, individual and group therapy supports, and medication management services. In helping families determine if these services would be helpful to them, ask them about their satisfaction with their current child psychiatry team. This becomes crucial because in many states participation in a therapeutic school environment *and* an outpatient child psychiatric facility *might* be considered duplication of services. Families may need to choose one over the other.

Hospital-Based Instruction

These are instructional services provided to the child during an acute psychiatric or some other type of hospitalization. Obviously, education might not be considered the priority during hospitalization. Still, there are often licensed teachers available in hospitals to provide educational support regardless of whether the child is being treated for a psychiatric condition or other health disorder.

Residential Programs

Residential programs represent another kind of "restrictive environment." These programs are for students whose complex needs cannot be met in a day program. Enrollment in these programs requires significant documentation of extraordinary needs and circumstances as evidenced by the following:

- A history of multiple hospitalizations
- A lack of responsiveness to intensive home- and community-based services, treatments, and interventions
- A pattern of emotional and educational decline despite the potential to succeed in school
- A safety concern due to sexualized or promiscuous behaviors, often associated with trauma and/or sexual abuse

There are many types of residential programs across the country. The following is a brief listing of possibilities. Check with your state agencies to determine what is available in your area.

Dually Licensed Residential Programs

There are several different options for how a residential program can be dually licensed, as shown in Table 14.1. How a program is licensed often determines the system through which a student's enrollment is processed. Dual licenses have two sets of criteria that must be fulfilled for a student to participate. It is important to research and find out about these programs and their criteria in your state.

Generally, only the state mental health system licenses residential treatment facilities. These are residential programs that focus solely or mainly on mental health treatment. Parents can initiate the process of applying to these programs for intensive therapeutic interventions in a residential setting through their child's psychiatrist. This application process is lengthy and must include involvement of a team that will help assess the child and verify the need for this intense level of instruction and/or services delivery.

As a parent advisor, you must check each child service system (such as the Department of Mental Health, Department of Mental Retardation and Developmental Delays, Department of Social Services, Department of Juvenile Justice, and so on) to identify what residential options are available for families

Table 14.1 *Dual License Options for Residential Programs*

Option 1:	State Office of Mental Health and the State Office of Education	Usually processed through the education system
Option 2:	State Department of Social Service (DSS) and the State Office of Education	Usually processed through a voluntary placement with the Child Welfare Unit of the DSS
Option 3:	State Office of Education and the State Department of Social Service (DSS)	Usually processed through the school system
Option 4 :	State Department of Social Services, State Department of Juvenile Justice, and the State Office of Education	Usually processed through the Juvenile Justice and/or Family Court System

in your area. Regardless of the options or your location in the country, *all* residential programs require proof that nothing else has worked. The application must include documentation from the community schools and services the family has tried. It must also show how the student's emotional stability *and academic achievement* have not been responsive to these local services, classes, and interventions. This comprehensive application packet usually includes the following:

- Psychosocial history
- Psychiatric evaluation with a rationale for a residential setting
- Psychological or neuropsychological evaluation
- Education evaluation
- Other relevant evaluations (occupational, speech and language, and so on)
- Documentation from previous providers
- Educational anecdotal information
- Physical
- Comprehensive listing of previous schools, programs, services, and so on

How Can Parents Get Additional Assistance?

Many parents find themselves automatically placed into the role of being an advocate for their child's education. Yet they may not have sufficient information about appropriate laws and available services. To aid parents in this position, school districts and state education offices have developed materials for parents. These materials can help parents become better informed and more knowledgeable about services and how to access them.

In addition, parent support and education programs have developed around the country to assist parents in being informed advocates for their child's education. Local school districts, community organizations, parent resource centers, federal parent organizations with state and local chapters, or other state parent organizations can all provide parents with support beyond your working relationship. Connecting families to these communities can help them help themselves in the long run and position them to help other families as well. Do not forget the local library and the wealth of information available on the Internet. Your state's or local region's Web site often includes valuable information.

See Appendix A for a list of useful Web sites and helpful organizations. Encourage parents to contact these organizations to educate themselves about the available services and their child's rights and entitlements.

Self-Study

After reviewing this chapter, ask yourself the following questions:

1. What is the purpose of special education?

2. What are some common types of special education programs?

3. What other restrictive educational placements may be available?

4. What is a good strategy to use if a student excels in one or more subjects?

5. What is required for access to residential programs?

6. What is the difference between homeschooling and home instruction?

7. How can I help parents get additional assistance?

Part IV

Education Laws Families
Should Know

Overview of Federal
Education Laws

RueZalia Watkins

All the services provided in a school come from state government or through the states from the federal government. A child's right to a sound, basic education is *not* a right or entitlement supported by the U.S. Constitution. However, there have been and currently are many federal laws that support education and instruction for many different kinds of students. Further, education and a child's right to it are part of every state's constitution. Whether an art class, physics class, guidance counseling, instruction, books, or lunch, all education services in the public schools come from state law and are supported by state and/or federal funds.

Education as we know it is the responsibilities of states and local municipalities. That is why it is important as a parent advisor to use state resources, identify state processes, and communicate with state offices. State resources are also very helpful in keeping up with federal laws. As federal laws are reauthorized, they may change in their intent, name, or purpose. *Reauthorization* is a term used for the process of renewing a federal law. The process begins with a congressional review of the status, successes, and weaknesses of the law. Then the proposed changes are incorporated into a renewed version of the law. When a federal law is created or reauthorized, the states have to write regulations to adopt it and establish guidelines to implement it. See Appendix A for Web sites providing information on education laws.

This chapter looks at several federal laws that provide instructional services and supports for students. The five pieces of federal legislation that direct or impact education to the states are the No Child Left Behind Act, the Individuals With Disabilities Education Improvement Act, Section 504 of the

Rehabilitation Act, the McKinney Vento Education of the Homeless Act, and the Combating Autism Act. In reading this chapter, try to review one law at a time.

History of Federal Education Law and Policy

It may be helpful, however, to first take a brief journey through the history of federal education law and policy. This will give you a better idea of its relationship to and influence from the states.

Federal Legislation Time Line: 1946–2004

1946   Federally subsidized school lunch program.

1950   Legislation passed to provide unregulated financial assistance to schools and communities called "impact grants."

1953   Creation of the U.S. Department of Health, Education, and Welfare.

1955–1958   School construction bills failed to pass because *Brown v. Brown* created requirement for all federal funds to schools to promote desegregation.

1956   Legislation passed to support teacher-training programs, diagnostic equipment for hearing and vision tests, and vocational rehabilitation facilities.

1957   Bills passed to provide more books for blind students and support for creating advanced special education teacher-training programs in colleges and universities.

1958   Emergency vote for the National Defense Education Act carried to provide science, math, engineering, and foreign language instruction and materials to improve student achievement in these areas.

1963   Maternal and Child Health and Mental Retardation Planning Act granted $265 million to develop programs for the mentally challenged.
The Mental Retardation Facilities and Community Mental Health Construction Act granted funds to construct buildings to serve the disabled.
The Manpower Development and Training Act supported vocational education for at-risk high school students and adults.
The Juvenile Delinquency and Youth Offenses Control Act funded programs to cut dropout rates, improve academic skills, and provide counseling to low-income students.

Vocational Education Act collapsed other vocational legislation into a comprehensive bill.

1965   Elementary and Secondary Education Act—Title I focused on needs of the poorest students, Title II sent resources for libraries, Title III supported foreign language instruction, Title IV provided funding for teacher professional development, and Title V provided funding to expand the individual state education departments.

1967   Title VII added to Elementary and Secondary Education Act for bilingual education.

1969   Elementary and Secondary Education Act Amendments including the addition of parent participation, which is the beginning of parent involvement in school decision making.

1972   Higher Education Act Reauthorization including the development of the National Institute of Education.

1973   Rehabilitation Act, which includes Section 504.

1974   Reauthorization of Elementary and Secondary Education Act to give aid to special education.
Bilingual Education Act amended.
Juvenile Justice and Delinquency Act.

1975   Education for All Handicapped Children Act increased aid to the schools for special education.

1976   Vocational Education Amendments.

1979   Department of Education Organization Act allowed for federal office to be developed and supports for state offices as well.

1980   Refugee Education Assistance Act.

1981   Head Start Act—the beginning of early childhood education.

1982   Student financial assistance.

1984   Education for Economic Security Act.

1986   Anti Drug Abuse Act (Drug Free Schools 1988).

1987   McKinney-Vento Homeless Assistance Act.

1988   Education and Training for a Competitive America Act.

1990   Americans With Disabilities Act.

1992   Higher Education Facilities Act.
Higher-education amendments.

1994   Reauthorization of Elementary Secondary Education Act becomes the Improving America's School Act.

1994   School to Work Opportunity Act jointly administered by the Departments of Education and Labor to provide experience for high school and post–high school students.

1997	Individuals With Disabilities Education Act.
1998	Carl D Perkins Vocational and Technical Education Act provides support for higher education and vocational supports, mostly through subsidized loans.
2000	Goals 2000 Educate America Act legislated six national goals to create education strategies based on standards set by the business community.
2001	No Child Left Behind Act (reauthorization of Elementary and Secondary Education Act).
2002	Richard B. Russell (National School Lunch Act of 1946) Amendments.
2004	Individuals With Disabilities Education Improvement Act.

This time line allows us to understand the past and how we can be part of the future. Today's strategies and laws can be viewed like others in the past and others to come. This time line gives us a sense that laws will always be developed, modified, and/or reauthorized.

All current federal laws are administered through your state. Some of these laws provide funding, but not all. Keep in mind that not every state has federal education offices to monitor services or provide resources. These tasks are fulfilled by your local state education department, which in turn provides services and supports to your local county, district, city, township, borough, or other area.

No Child Left Behind Act (Elementary and Secondary Education Act—Title I)

The first thing parents need to know about the No Child Left Behind Act (NCLB) is that it affects all students, whether they have special needs or not. However, while the act provides for enhanced instruction to *all* students, it provides for supplemental services and school choice to only *some* students. The NCLB requires all students across America in grades 3 to 8 to take standardized tests in reading and math. In the future, this may be extended to math students in high school as well. These tests are administered by the states. States have to prove to the federal government that their students are achieving, regardless of race, ethnicity, language, grade, location, and socioeconomic or disabling conditions. For example, even disabled students who are legally allowed to use a calculator on tests are not allowed to use one for the NCLB math test. This is to ensure that students are being taught to calculate and perform mathematical tasks.

NCLB and Title I

Many parents may remember the term Title I. This term was used to describe a range of services to improve instruction and outcomes for students. Title I is actually the first section of the Elementary and Secondary Education Act (ESEA). Title II related to the second section of the act, Title III related to the third section act, and so on. The primary aim of Title I was to provide services that targeted instruction in order to help students achieve. It also established a process to ensure that these services were working. These services were to be provided to the neediest students, especially students living in poverty. The NCLB is the reauthorization of ESEA (see time line).

Specifics of NCLB

The NCLB charges states with the responsibility to ensure the following for *all* public school students in the state regardless of age, dominant language, ethnicity, geographic location, and/or disabling condition:

- Early identification of learning problems
- Highly qualified teachers in licensed areas
- Research-based academic interventions
- Professional development for teachers and school staff
- Parental involvement in all school processes
- Parent training on education-related topics
- Parental participation in school decision making
- Statewide tests to document *all* students' progress
- Safety transfers for students
- Annual target numbers for schools to make consistent progress
- Documented annual progress for low-performing schools

The following additional services are available to *some* students:

- Supplemental education services for students with need
- School choice

Supplementary education services are tutoring services usually provided by an outside company. Students have to meet state eligibility guidelines to get these services. It must be apparent from the standardized testing that the school has failed to meet a child's educational needs. Check your state's Web site or speak with your state liaison to see what test scores and other criteria must be met for a student to qualify for these services.

Additionally, there are separate guidelines to access the school-choice option. This option may allow children to enroll in a better school than their current one. Only when schools have documented their inability to meet the academic needs of students and failed to meet their own school annual yearly progress targets will parents have access to the choice option.

Finding More Information on NCLB

You can help the families you are working with find out if their child's school is performing up to par. Information on the status of schools in your area can be found through your state's Web site or the state education department representative for your area. Your state or local education office can tell you which schools are successful and which may be low performing or failing. This practice of evaluating schools has really been in existence since the establishment of the Elementary Education and Secondary Education Act in the 1960s. The NCLB makes this information more accessible. You can also find information about a school's academic track record in your local paper when the annual results to federal and state tests are published. It is important that you collect this information and general information on NCLB from the many education offices in your area by visiting your state's Web site and visiting the offices in person. It would be very helpful for you to have a listing of the schools most impacted by NCLB in your area. This information is helpful in assisting families as they choose or reject a placement for their special needs child. Make sure to keep this list updated, as the status of schools changes every year. This change usually happens in the summer when the year's tests results are publicized.

Individuals With Disabilities Education Improvement Act

While NCLB is designed to ensure educational excellence for all students, the Individuals With Disabilities Education Improvement Act (IDEIA) provides for the education of special needs students. The two work together to ensure access and accountability for every student.

The IDEIA, passed in 2004, is the reauthorization of the Individuals With Disabilities Education Act (IDEA) of 1997. (In many states, it is still called IDEA, but the short title after this most recent reauthorization adds the additional "I" for "Improvement.") It is important for us to remember that special education is supposed to be improving education outcomes for our children. The IDEA law guaranteed a free and appropriate public education for children. It also detailed the due process procedures that we now rely on to develop an Individual Education Plan (IEP). (See Chapter 16 for more information on the IEP process.) The way states carry out this law can vary from state to state, but all states have to adopt and implement the basic requirements of the federal statute. Many states are just now beginning to make changes in response to the reauthorization of this law. Every state can choose to have higher standards or broader guidelines. You must check with your individual state to see how this new legislation will be put into effect.

Specifics of IDEIA

Most of the special education processes encompassed under the original IDEA legislation remain the same under the new reauthorization. This includes the IEP process and many of the types of services that a student can receive. Thus, whatever ways you were helping families access services through an IEP will not change with the exception of the following:

- School districts are no longer required to use a detailed discrepancy between the student's intellectual potential and academic achievement to determine if a learning disability exists. In the past, school districts would measure the difference between these numbers, and if the difference was 50% or more, it would imply the presence of a learning disorder. Specific learning disabilities may no longer be identified solely through this method. Depending on your state's guidelines, it may be necessary to provide evidence of a specific learning disorder through separate evaluations. For example, a child may have to undergo speech and language, auditory processing, or perceptual evaluations to best document learning disorders.
- The law also requires proof that the interventions and strategies recommended in an evaluation work and will help the student succeed. This concept is called *response to interventions,* and it is used as part of the evaluation process and program implementation.
- States and districts can use other means to determine if students have special learning needs. For example, a student's response to scientifically based learning interventions (response to intervention) can be used as a basis to establish special learning needs.
- Schools and districts can now use special education funds to screen students for academic or learning deficiencies. A percentage of special education funds can be used to provide research-based instructional interventions to screened students in small groups before they are offered special education services.
- Depending on your state plan, a child may *not* have short-term objectives toward meeting an annual goal on the child's IEP. The IEPs for children with developmental delays, however, still require short-term objectives.

- The time from evaluation to placement for students who have never had special education services in the past is now 60 days total. Previously, this time was divided in half, giving the school system 30 days to evaluate a new special education candidate and another 30 days to classify and place. For example, a school system can now take 45 days to evaluate a student and classify him or her and recommend placement within the balance of time (15 days). This change applies only to students who have never received special education services.

- The IDEIA now allows students with disabilities to be suspended for 10 to 45 days *and* placed in an alternative setting *with services,* provided that the services were already on the IEP. The law also requires schools to follow strict procedures in disciplining and suspending students with disabilities. Some of these are listed under positive changes of the law. Check with your state and local school district regarding discipline procedures and suspension processes.

- Annual reviews may be optional. This depends not only on your state but also on the view of the parents and other appropriate parties as to whether changes to the IEP are necessary. If a student is progressing well with the existing IEP, then there may not be a need for an annual review to suggest changes.

- Due process options to request an impartial hearing (see next point) when parents disagree with a school system decision are now diluted by adding layers of prehearing meetings called resolution meetings. These are mandated mediation meetings designed to resolve differences between the parents and the school system before an impartial hearing is scheduled. Many states have different time frames; often, resolution meetings must be scheduled within 15 business days, so check with your state office. If there is no agreement to "resolve" the difference of opinion regarding the educational issue for the student, an impartial hearing is scheduled.

- Impartial hearings are formal legal proceedings generated when families and the school system do not agree about some facet of special education, including identification, classification, evaluation, service delivery, education program, and/or placement. In this legal process, a hearing officer is assigned to resolve the difference of opinion regarding the issue. Hearing officers are appointed by the state and often the commissioner of education for the state to preside over this legally binding process, which both sides are able to present their view regarding the education dilemma. Parents are allowed to have an attorney whose fees may or may not be reimbursable by the state (check with your state regulations). The hearing officer must determine whether the student's legal entitlements according to state implementation of IDEIA have been or would be violated by the proposed actions of the person requesting the impartial hearing or defending his or her position within the hearing process. It is best to seek specific information regarding your state's due process regulations detailing the impartial hearing definitions, terms, time frames, the number of issues that can be addressed in one hearing, and other legal questions and procedures.

Some of the more positive changes in the law include the following:

- Teachers must be highly qualified to teach the core subject areas to students receiving special education services. In high school, this means that teachers may need to be dually certified in special education and in the core subject area, or there may have to be two teachers in the high school classroom, one certified in the subject area and another certified in special education instruction.
- Students will be held to the same academic standards as their nondisabled peers, preventing a dual class education system.
- Transition services are strengthened in the law by listing specific services that must be included in a transition plan and detailing when a transition IEP must be developed.
- Manifestation determination hearings are required to determine if a student's behavior is a "manifestation" of the disabling condition (i.e., related to student's disability). Functional behavior assessments must also be conducted and behavior intervention plans developed before a student with a disability can be suspended for more than 10 days.
- Incentives have been created for early childhood programs and positive behavioral intervention services (PBIS) for entire school communities.
- States are required to report on the overrepresentation of children of color in restricted special education settings.
- States are also required to gather feedback from families regarding special education processes, including communication, as part of a monitoring process required by the federal government to ensure quality in practices involving families of special needs children.
- Principals and other school personnel cannot refuse educational access if parents choose not to give their child medication for a behavioral, emotional, or other mental health condition. Whether a child takes medication is a decision to be made between the family and their child's doctors.
- Because IEPs are now portable around the country, students will not have to stay out of school waiting for evaluations because the family moved to a new location.

Section 504 of the Rehabilitation Act

Another federal law that can help provide services for students with special needs is Section 504 of the Rehabilitation Act. The Rehabilitation Act is a huge law with many different sections. The law provides for training, education, regular and vocational rehabilitation, preparation for work, as well as access to programs for all individuals with disabilities. Specifically, Section 504 of this act states that an organization must offer whatever services or accommodations that children (or adults) with documented impairments need to fully participate with their nondisabled peers, provided that the organization accepts federal funding of any type.

Here are two examples of federal funding that would allow families to seek Section 504 services for their children:

- A private school that accepts lunch services from the U.S. Department of Agriculture—Free Lunch Program
- A secular/religious school that accepts external science lab buses given by the local education department and funded by Title XI of the ESEA

In both examples, students with disabilities would have to be given whatever accommodations they need to participate in the federally funded program with their nondisabled peers. Section 504 can be used with recreational programs, creative programs, college programs, and any other program, provided that they accept some form of federal funding.

Note that private and religious schools that are not receiving funds from the federal government are not required to comply with Section 504. In this case, families would have to contact their local committee on special education to pursue special education services through IDEIA, which can be given while a child is in a private setting.

Specifics of Section 504

Children who are allowed to use Section 504 are those who have physical or mental conditions that significantly limit at least one major life activity, such as learning, dressing, socializing, and even playing. In order to provide a suitable education to a child, an accommodation plan can be developed for adjustments in a regular classroom. Some generalized accommodations are listed here, though specific adjustments should be individualized for each child:

- Modified homework assignments and testing
- Supervision of homework assignments

- Reduction in the amount of written work and/or extended deadline to complete any assignments
- Access to a computer for written work if easier
- Alternate seating arrangements in the classroom (i.e., closer to teacher or away from hallway noise)
- Use of helpful tools (calculator, tape recorder, or electronic spell checker)
- Continual progress reports assessing behavior and/or assignments
- Behavioral intervention plan/social skills training
- Test accommodations

Once it is clear what accommodations a medical doctor feels a child needs to function and participate in a program, a Section 504 plan is created. Section 504 plans are not ongoing. They are good for 1 year and must be re-created and resubmitted every year, regardless of whether they are for elementary school, after-school programs, or college. (See Chapter 16 for more information on using a Section 504 plan.)

McKinney-Vento Act for the Education of Homeless Children and Youth

In every school district and/or region, there is a professional responsible for ensuring that homeless children receive a free and appropriate education. The McKinney-Vento Act uses the following to define homeless students:

- Students who lack a fixed, regular, and adequate nighttime residence and includes students who are

  - sharing the housing of other persons because of a loss of housing for any reason,
  - living in hotels, motels, trailer parks, or campgrounds because of a lack of adequate accommodations,
  - living in emergency or transitional shelters,
  - abandoned in hospitals, or
  - awaiting foster care placement.

- Students who have a primary nighttime residence that is a public or private place not designed for use as regular sleeping accommodations for human beings.

- Students who are living in cars, parks, public spaces, abandoned buildings, substandard housing, bus or train stations, and so on
- Migratory children who qualify as homeless because they are living in the circumstances listed previously.

There are three important things to remember about this act:

1. Remember the definition and make sure that any child living in these situations has full protection under this law.
2. One of these protections is the child's entitlement to continue his or her education in the school of origin, even when it requires transportation. Another example of an entitlement under this act is funding for books and clothes.
3. These students also have entitlements covered under all other federal education laws: IDEIA, Section 504 of the Rehabilitation Act, and the NCLB. Entitlements under NCLB include access to Title I funds to pay for some of the additional expenses these children may have.

The Combating Autism Act of 2006

This is the first piece of legislation that begins to address the distinct needs of children with autism and their families. This act enhances research, surveillance, and education regarding autism spectrum disorders; however, all the education provisions for students with autism are still provided through IDEIA. Although this is not a comprehensive piece of legislation, it is still a welcomed beginning for expanding awareness of autism spectrum disorders and will generate information throughout the country to help families. Specifically, this act gives the U.S. secretary of education the responsibility to establish regional centers to perform the following:

- Provide information and education on autism spectrum disorders and other developmental disabilities to increase public awareness of developmental milestones
- Promote research into the development and validation of reliable screening tools for autism spectrum disorders and other developmental disabilities and disseminate information regarding those screening tools
- Promote early screening of individuals at higher risk for autism spectrum disorders and other developmental disabilities as early as practicable
- Increase the number of individuals who are able to confirm or rule out a diagnosis of autism spectrum disorders and other developmental disabilities
- Increase the number of individuals able to provide evidence-based interventions for individuals diagnosed with autism spectrum disorders or other developmental disabilities
- Promote the use of evidence-based interventions for individuals at higher risk for autism spectrum disorders and other developmental disabilities as early as practicable

Self-Study

After reviewing this chapter, ask yourself the following questions:

1. What level of the government is responsible for a child's education?

2. What are some of the services provided for by NCLB?

3. What are some of the changes to the law under IDEIA?

4. What kinds of programs are affected by Section 504?

5. How is "homelessness" defined by the McKinney-Vento Act?

6. How will the Combating Autism Act help families?

7. Which of these laws will you use and how?

Individual Education Plan
Versus Section 504 Plan

RueZalia Watkins

A s parents seek services for their child, an important part of your job will
be helping them understand how to request and use an Individual Education Plan (IEP) or a Section 504 plan. Both processes can be used to access
school services for students with special needs. Part IV of this book provides
more information on specific services available. This chapter focuses on the
differences between these two approaches and the procedures for using them
to get help for students.

The Individuals With Disabilities Education Improvement Act versus Section 504

First, it is important to take another look at the two significant federal laws
that generate these plans. The IEP is provided for by the Individuals With Disabilities Education Improvement Act (IDEIA). Section 504 plans are generated
through the Rehabilitation Act.

IDEIA

Provides a free and appropriate public education for all children between the
ages of 3 and 21 who have a disabling condition, including mental illness, and
who attend an early intervention or pre-K through high school program.

Section 504 of the Rehabilitation Act of 1973

Provides the services and/or accommodations individuals with disabling conditions require to ensure full participation, complete access, and equal opportunity within organizations (including schools) and programs that accept
any type of federal funding.

Every child who is a student with a disability under IDEIA is also protected under Section 504. However, not all children covered under Section 504 are necessarily students with a disability under IDEIA. This is because eligibility for IDEIA requires that a child be classified as having a disability requiring special education services through the school system. Eligibility for Section 504 occurs when a child needs an accommodation in any federally funded program, whether it is part of a school or not. Children who have less severe disabilities that require minimal accommodations and who are otherwise not eligible for IDEIA may be covered under Section 504.

The Section 504 process does require that an evaluation be conducted before a child receives a 504 plan and before any accommodations are provided or alterations made to the plan. However, Section 504 places far fewer rules and regulations on the testing process than IDEIA. For example, Section 504:

- *does not* require several separate evaluations, such as an education evaluation
- *does not* require parent consent for testing, unless it is required by the family's doctor who is preparing the information for the Section 504 plan

Since Section 504 provides less strict safeguards, you should be aware that certain situations may arise that the 504 plan would not cover. For example, a 504 plan could not provide a "stay-put" provision to keep the child in his or her current educational placement while any issues between the family and the school are being resolved through due process activities. If a student's needs cannot be addressed through a Section 504 plan, a family might have to complete a comprehensive evaluation process and access services through IDEIA using an IEP.

It is also important to note that, in most schools, 504 plans do not continue with the child to the next grade. In these cases, a 504 plan must be renewed or re-created each year. Table 16.1 describes some of the other major differences between these significant laws.

Creating a 504 Plan

Section 504 is a civil rights law, so depending on the location, parents can contact either the local school district, the state education department, or the civil rights office to ask questions to determine if this law is applicable to their child. Most of the time, the local school district is the most expedient. Since each school district handles 504 plans differently, it is important to connect

Table 16.1 *IDEIA Versus Section 504*

Provision/Description	*Section 504*	*IDEIA (IEP)*
Requires evaluations to document need for services	Yes, a medical doctor makes the recommendations	Yes, the school does a comprehensive evaluation
Requires parental consent for testing through the school system to determine what a student needs	No, unless required by the medical doctors preparing the 504 plan	Yes, since the school system determines eligibility for services
Requires education evaluations	No	Yes
Requires a psychological evaluation	Yes, if relevant to the disorder	Yes
Requires speech and language evaluations	Yes, if relevant to the disorder	Yes, if relevant to the disorder
Requires an occupational or perceptual evaluation	Yes, if relevant to the disorder	Yes, if relevant to the disorder
Provides services in a general education setting	Yes	Yes
Legally documents a child's disabling condition to ensure ongoing and consistent access to special services and accommodations	No	Yes
Provides discipline safeguards before a student can be suspended	No	Yes
Requires the development of an IEP	Yes, in some schools and areas	Yes
Requires the development of a 504 plan	Yes	No
Allows testing accommodations for all grades including 12th grade of high school	Yes	Yes

continued

Provision/Description	Section 504	IDEIA (IEP)
Allows testing accommodations for all grades including college	Yes, pending federal funding	No, provides testing accommodations only for grades K through 12
Allows testing accommodations for SAT precollege examinations	No	Yes, requires high school IEP
Maintains placement in a program or school with a specific classification pending hearing decision (pendancy)	No	Yes
Allows families to use an IEP anywhere in the country without waiting for new evaluations before a student can receive services in a new school district	No	Yes

families to the local education offices where they can find help. In many local education offices, those responsible for Section 504 activities are health officers; in other areas, they are part of the support staff.

Parents should put their request for a 504 plan in writing. They should date and sign a letter that explains the reason for the request by indicating the concerns, problem areas, and/or issues to be addressed. Some schools have forms for these "request for referral" letters. Parents should take extra copies of the form to share with the child's doctors as needed. They should also make a copy of the letter they will submit to the school for their own records. It is best, if possible, to personally give the original to the child's school. On delivery, the school is required to begin an evaluation process following strict and clearly defined guidelines. This evaluation process includes a review of the medical documentation that families are required to provide from their child's doctor. This documentation should state what services and supports are needed for the child and why. Keep in mind that guidelines and procedures for processing and developing a 504 plan may differ. Make sure that parents ask their schools or local school districts for this information.

Example of Student Accommodation Plan

Student: <u>John Doe</u>   School: <u>Jefferson</u>

Date of Birth: <u>10/15/94</u>   Grade: <u>8</u>

1. *Describe the nature of the concern(s):*
   John does not return his homework assignments. John has difficulty with organization of class work and pacing of assignments. He's easily distracted by extraneous stimuli and has difficulty listening to lecture and taking notes at the same time.

2. *Describe the bases for the determination of disability:*
   John was diagnosed 3 years ago as having attention-deficit/hyperactivity disorder.

3. *Describe how the disability affects a major life activity:*
   John's multidisciplinary team indicated that he has difficulty with day dreaming and staying on task at school. He is failing two classes because he has not turned in his homework.

4. *Describe the services and/or accommodations that are necessary:*
   John's teachers will provide a weekly schedule of John's assignments 1 week in advance. John will be given one copy, and one copy will be mailed to his parents. John will be seated near the front of the room in close proximity to the teacher. John's parents will provide NCR (carbonless copy) paper so that a classmate can take notes and immediately give John a copy of the notes—or the teacher will provide a copy of the lecture notes.

Review/Reassessment Date: <u>November 3, 2008</u>

Participants:	*Title:*
John Doe	Student
Kristy Long	English Teacher
Jim Johnson	Assistant Principal/504 Coordinator
Connie Murphy	School Counselor
Sarah Petes	Social Studies Teacher
Jane Doe	Mother

If a child is deemed eligible under Section 504, the school district must develop a Section 504 plan. This plan will include possible accommodations as previously described. It is important to remember that unlike the IEP process, regulations for Section 504 do not specify the frequency of review of the plan or the role of outside evaluations. They also do not require parental involvement. However, encourage parents to be involved with every step of the process. In addition, parents should request that the accommodations decided on be placed in writing and signed by all parties involved within the school and family. Copies can then be given to the child's doctor and maintained in the family and school records as well.

In some cases, Section 504 plans automatically generate IEP plans to ensure continuity of services and funding for the staff that may be required to implement the services in the plan. If Section 504 plans are not connected to IEPs in a family's school district, you should remind parents that they will have to revisit the Section 504 process when their child goes to the next grade.

IDEIA Process

Many parents will decide to utilize the IDEIA process as opposed to the Section 504 process. It will be helpful for you to become familiar with every aspect of this law and how it is implemented in your state. It is also important for you to learn about all of the services that are available to students in a general education setting under these provisions (see Chapter 13). After the evaluation process, you can provide parents with a clearer picture of the services their child may need and how to access them with an IEP. All services through IDEIA are based on evaluations; therefore, it is important to know what evaluations are available and the best way to get them.

Evaluation Procedure

The first step is to help families contact the school and express their concerns about their child. The school may be able to create a temporary action or intervention plan for a child while the evaluations are being performed and the IEP is being developed. Temporary action or intervention plans are usually created by a team within the school that may include members of the special education team, but these plans are not created by the special education team (see Table 16.2).

To start the special education process, the case is referred to the team solely responsible for special education in the school. This referral will start a series

Table 16.2 *Educational Planning Teams*

Team	*Members*	*Responsibilities*
School support team— non-special education	Principal Guidance counselor Parent Teacher Parent advisor	Produces a temporary intervention plan for students who are having difficulty but are not classified. Services may include behavior management, counseling, time-outs, or some tutoring.
School-based special education team	School psychologists Education evaluator (optional) Social worker Teacher Parent Parent team member	Produces an IEP to give special education services in a general education setting or a special education setting in the existing school or another school in the district.
Local district-based special education committee	District psychologist Education evaluator (optional) Social worker Special education teacher Classroom teacher Parent team member Parent	Produces an IEP like the school-based team, but this team usually has the authority to recommend special education placement in a day treatment program, non–public school, hospital, or residential program. Usually, the regional team must approve these recommendations.
Regional-based special education team	Often this team does not meet with the parent; rather, they talk with the parent on the phone, suggest programs, and provide access for visits to programs as part of the selection process.	Basic function is to secure the funding approval (usually from the state) and to find a private, residential, day treatment, or hospital setting for the child.

of evaluations and tests, requiring parents' written consent. These evaluations will determine what the child's strengths and weaknesses are, what his or her grade levels are in reading and math, why the child is having difficulty, what services the child needs to improve, when the child needs to receive them, and what modifications are required to ensure the child reaches his or her academic potential. Parents are entitled to have copies of these evaluations when they are completed. In the rare event that the school denies testing, parents have the right to appeal the decision.

The components of the evaluation process are described on the following pages. You should have a firm understanding of each of these evaluations and their differences in order to be able to explain them to parents. Also, your aim is to reduce fears, stigma, and the negative feelings many families have about evaluations and the special education process.

Social History: All evaluations begin with meeting the parents to document the family structure, home environment, and major occurrences in the child's life and/or the life of the family. Evaluators also gather information from the parents on the child's physical development, emotional history, school history, social life, hobbies, interests, challenges, and strengths. It is of particular importance to discuss the child's strengths with the parents beforehand to help them effectively communicate these during the interview. This will help ensure that the student's existing interests and abilities are not ignored because of psychological, attention, or learning problems. This will allow the strategies within the IEP to incorporate and build on the subject areas in which the child excels. For example, a student who excels in math may be mainstreamed in a general education math class or skipped to the next level.

Psychological Evaluation: A comprehensive psychological evaluation will be conducted unless the child has had a recent private evaluation that was submitted to the school psychologist. This evaluation includes several different tests that measure a child's intelligence, academic achievement levels, perceptual and language processing and speed, and ability to complete tasks within a certain time frame. These tests will also determine the child's preferred method of learning, that is, whether the child is a visual learner or learns through hearing or learns only by doing things with his or her hands. These tests allow the psychologist to make specific recommendations about the services and accommodations the child needs to achieve in the academic setting. If a child has a mental illness or learning problem, other tests are necessary.

In most states, a comprehensive psychological evaluation is valid for 3 years and will not be redone within 1 year.

Psychiatric or Neurological Evaluations: If a child has a mental illness or neurological disorder such as attention-deficit/hyperactivity disorder, an evaluation from a psychiatrist or a neurologist will be necessary. A child's psychiatrist may perform this evaluation, or the school system can refer parents to a licensed child psychiatrist. This evaluation will include a questionnaire for parents to fill out about the child's functioning at home and at school as well as another questionnaire for the child's teacher to submit. This evaluation will include recommendations such as medications, therapy, or counseling as well as suggestions for the school environment (e.g., time-out breaks during the school day).

Education Evaluation: It is usually best for the school system to perform this battery of tests to ensure that the results are compatible with the testing standards within the school system. Tests given include spelling, decoding, writing, reading, comprehension, arithmetic, and mathematical word problems. Education evaluators also note how the child listens, follows directions, holds a pencil, and completes tasks in a timely manner to determine if other tests are necessary. It is crucial to make sure that this evaluation looks not only at deficits but at the child's "best subjects" as well.

Speech and Language Evaluations: If parents or the evaluators find a child has problems with spelling, reading, speaking in whole sentences, following verbal directions, or any other mainly language-based problems, separate tests may be given to examine language functioning. A child may have a problem processing what he or she hears or a problem following and remembering words and numbers on a page. A speech and language evaluation gives information regarding the source of these types of difficulties and determines what services are necessary to help the student improve. The evaluation should include proof that these services and strategies will work. This evaluation should also include how often the services should be given, whether they should be given alone or in a small group, how long each speech and language session should be, and in what type of setting services should be given and for what duration within the school year.

Visual-Perceptual Evaluations: Parents may notice that their child has a problem with arithmetic, handwriting, spelling, reading, tying shoes, or completing other tasks that require coordination, such as throwing and catching a ball or riding a bicycle. In this case, there are tests that need to be administered by a specialist to determine if the child has a perceptual- or visual-based learning problem. This evaluation will give the specific information necessary to make detailed recommendations for services and supports to improve student achievement. An occupational therapy evaluation may also be recommended to see if occupational therapy, which helps with physical functioning, can help the child succeed with motor tasks. Sometimes occupational therapists help with organizational tasks. The evaluation should include the same specific recommendations as listed under the speech and language evaluations section.

Functional Behavior Assessments: If parents have a child who displays inappropriate and/or negative behaviors while in school, this form of testing can be very helpful. These assessments identify the behaviors in question and define them in specific terms, such as when they happen, where they happen, what time of day they are the most prevalent, what occurs before the behaviors, and what seems to help resolve the behavior. The results of these assessments are used in formulating the IEP, but most often they are used as part of behavior intervention plans and discipline processes. It is important to encourage families and schools to use these processes also with students who are reclusive and withdrawn rather than only with students who are disruptive. This will help students with depression, social phobias, anxieties, and so on receive specific interventions to help them to better adjust and function emotionally in the classroom.

Developing an IEP

Once a child has been evaluated, a meeting between the parents and the appropriate team will be scheduled. Teams are composed of members who are responsible for different types of services and belong to various parts of the education community. These teams are responsible for receiving and incorporating information from the family as well as reporting information to the family and working with them to develop a plan to address the child's needs. They are also mandated to work with the family to ensure that this plan also addresses a student's areas of prominence and achievement. Parents can bring a parent advisor—as well as other service providers or even a relative—to these meetings. In some areas, certain meetings may include a "parent team member." This member is a parent of a special needs child who has received special education services. Most often, they are employees of the school system; in some areas, they may be volunteers. However, families can still bring you to these meetings as well. Table 16.2 lists various teams, their members, and responsibilities.

Using an IEP

Once an IEP has been developed for the child, it is used to access specific services. The IEP must include following:

- Whether the services are provided one-on-one or in small groups
- What subject or other area is to be addressed
- Who is providing the service
- How often the services will be provided
- For what duration the services will be given
- When the services will be provided
- How long each service session will be
- What the goals of these services will be
- How these goals will be measured
- Who will measure these goals and how often
- What language will be used to provide services
- When the services will begin

The IEP carries over from one school year to the next. If the child moves and changes schools, the IEP follows him or her to the new school, and the IEP process need not be redone before the student receives services. The IEP process can be revisited if the new school district does not have the services that the old school district has; this is often the case when a family moves to another state. Also, states may call the same services by different names; so, if a family moves, the IEP may have to be translated or converted into the new state's language of service delivery. The bottom line is that no child will have to wait to attend school or receive services while a new evaluation process begins. The IEP can also be revisited if it is not working or if it is working so well that the student needs to be given access to a more challenging class, subject, or program. Not all children will need IEPs the rest of their academic lives. Often when students are given the special services they need, they can get to a level where they no longer need special education services; they may then need accommodations only for tests or nothing at all.

Self-Study

After reviewing this chapter, ask yourself the following questions:

1. What are some of the differences between IDEIA and Section 504 rules and regulations?

2. What are some cases of when an IEP should be used instead of a Section 504 plan?

3. What is necessary to create a Section 504 plan?

4. What are the different evaluations that are part the IDEIA process?

5. What are the different teams that may be involved in developing an IEP?

Appendix A: Resources

Advocacy Groups

There are several national family advocacy, support, and education organizations whose mission is to assist parents of children with mental health needs.

Federation of Families for Children's Mental Health

A national family-run organization that helps children with mental health needs and their families achieve a better quality of life through providing leadership to family-run organizations nationwide, working toward systems change, and assisting policymakers, agencies, and providers become more effective in delivering services and supports to families.

9605 Medical Center Dr., Suite 280
Rockville, MD 20850
Tel: 240–403–1901
Fax: 240–403–1909
E-mail: ffcmh@ffcmn.org
www.ffcmh.org

National Alliance on Mental Illness (NAMI)

The largest national grassroots mental health organization with the goal of eradicating mental illnesses and improving quality of life for those affected through support, education, advocacy, and research.

Colonial Place Three
2107 Wilson Blvd., Suite 300
Arlington, VA 22201–3042
Main: 703–524–7600
Fax: 703–524–9094
TDD: 703–516–7227
E-mail: info@nami.org
www.nami.org

Children and Adults With Attention Deficit/Hyperactivity Disorder (CHADD)

A national nonprofit organization that provides education, advocacy, and support for individuals with attention-deficit/hyperactivity disorder.

CHADD National Office
8181 Professional Pl., Suite 150
Landover, MD 20785
Tel: 301–306–7070
Fax: 301–306–7090
www.chadd.org

Mental Health America

A national nonprofit organization that promotes the message of mental health for all by educating the public on mental health issues as well as providing support and advocacy for individuals and families living with mental health and substance use problems.

2000 N. Beauregard St., 6th Floor
Alexandria, VA 22311
Tel: 703–684–7722
Fax: 703–684–5968
Toll free: 800–969–6642
TTY Line: 800–433–5959
www.mentalhealthamerica.net

Child and Adolescent Bipolar Foundation

This organization educates families, professionals, and the public about pediatric bipolar disorder; connects families with resources and support; advocates for and empowers affected families; and supports research on pediatric bipolar disorder and its cure.

1000 Skokie Blvd., Suite 570
Wilmette, IL 60091
cabf@bpkids.org
www.bpkids.org

Learning Disabilities Association of America (LDA)

The largest nonprofit volunteer association for individuals with learning disabilities whose mission is to support individuals affected by learning disabilities and reduce the incidence of learning disabilities in the future.

4156 Library Rd.
Pittsburgh, PA 15234–1349
Tel: 412–341–1515
Fax: 412–344–0224
www.ldaamerica.org

Training Programs

The following is a sampling of training programs offered nationally for parents and parent advisors.

Family Development Credential (FDC)

A 90-hour training program for family workers offered by Cornell University. Teaches how to coach low-income families to set and reach their own goals for healthy self-reliance. For more information, go to:

www.human.cornell.edu/che/HD/FDC

Family-to-Family Education Program

Free, 12-week course for family caregivers taught by trained family members. It provides information and teaches skills to help caregivers deal more effectively with family members with severe mental illness. For more information and access to additional training programs, go to:

www.nami.org/Template.cfm?Section=Family-to-Family&lstid=605

Federation Training Programs

Offers various training opportunities for parents involved with the mental health care system and for professionals working with families. For more information, go to:

www.ffcmh.org/training.htm

Parent to Parent: Family Training on ADHD

The curriculum, developed by parents and offered by Children and Adults with Attention Deficit/Hyperactivity Disorder (CHADD), provides information and support for individuals and families dealing with attention-deficit/hyperactivity disorder. The 14-hour course is offered locally across the country. For more information, go to:

www.chadd.org/AM/Template.cfm?Section=Parent_to_Parent_Program

The REACH Institute

Provides training for professionals, including the Parent Empowerment Program (PEP). See Appendix B for more information or go to:

www.reachinstitute.net/REACH_training.html

Web Resources

The following are some Web sites that offer an array of information on children's mental health topics.

National Dissemination Center for Children With Disabilities

For more information on various topics related to children and youth with disabilities, including special education laws, go to:

www.nichcy.org

Bridges 4 Kids—Building Partnerships Between Families, Schools, and Communities

For more information on education, mental health services, and insurance, go to:

www.bridges4kids.org/SSI.html

U.S. Department of Education

For more information on education laws, go to:

www.ed.gov

National Institute of Mental Health

For information on the full spectrum of mental health disorders, go to:

www.nimh.nih.gov

National Mental Health Information Center

Developed for users of mental health services and their families, the general public, policymakers, providers, and the media. For more information, go to:

http://mentalhealth.samhsa.gov

American Academy of Child and Adolescent Psychiatry

Includes information for families about developmental, behavioral, emotional, and mental disorders affecting children and adolescents. Go to:

www.aacap.org

Blueprints for Violence Prevention

A national violence prevention initiative to identify violence prevention programs that are effective. Go to:

www.colorado.edu/cspv/blueprints/index.html

The REACH Institute

For more information on disorder and treatment profiles, training in evidence-based practices, and resources for families, go to:

www.reachinstitute.net

Appendix B: About the Parent Empowerment Program

The Parent Empowerment Program (PEP) provides training for parent advisors and is administered by the Resource for Advancing Children's Health (REACH) Institute.

The PEP model was developed by a collaborative team that includes many of the developers of this guide, that is, parents, parent advisors, clinicians, and researchers. Each parent advisor training program is facilitated by a trained parents' advocate and mental health professional with experience in family support. The training program is designed to help participants develop their ability to work effectively with parents to acquire and participate in the best possible mental health services for their children. Drawing on the principles of behavior change described in the preface, the PEP training program involves two phases designed to enhance abilities in parent engagement and empowerment.

The first phase consists of 40 hours of training. These sessions include didactic training, practice exercises, and group discussion. Phase 1 is an opportunity to process key information from this guide. It teaches strategies to be implemented in the second phase.

The second phase consists of monthly follow-up sessions. Parent advisors are given the opportunity to practice applying their newly acquired knowledge, skills, and strategies in their work settings. They receive additional consultation from their trainers and peers. Phase 2 is viewed as critical to incorporating the training into practice. It involves activities for working with parents and delivering information to them.

Trainings are typically delivered over 10 weeks with 4-hour sessions (phase 1). The monthly consultation period (phase 2) generally lasts for 6 months to a year. Therefore, a time commitment is necessary for participation. The size of the group is kept small (5–12 people) in order to best meet the goals and individual needs of each participant.

Training is available nationally. Parent advisors interested in becoming trained in PEP should contact the REACH Institute directly at:

The REACH Institute
71 West 23rd Street
8th Floor
New York, NY 10010
Phone: 212-845-4486 or 212-845-4606
Fax: 917-438-0894
Email: info@thereachinstitute.org.
www.reachinstitute.net

Appendix C: Index of Parent Handouts and Important Points for Parent Advisors

Parent Handouts

Important Points for Parent Advisors

References

Ajzen, I., & Fishbein, M. (1981). *Understanding attitudes and predicting social behavior.* Englewood Cliffs, NJ: Prentice Hall.

Amador, X. F., & Johanson, A. L. (2000). *I am Not Sick I Don't Need Help!: Helping the Seriously Mentally Ill Accept Treatment* (Paperback ed.). New York: Vida Press.

American Psychiatric Association. (2000). *Diagnostic and statistical manual of mental disorders* (text revision). Washington, DC: Author.

Assistance to states for the education of children with disabilities, 34 C.F.R. § 300.8 (2007).

Bickman, L., Heflinger, C. A., Northrup, D., Sonnichsen, S., & Schilling, S. (1998). Long-term outcomes to family caregiver empowerment. *Journal of Child and Family Studies, 7,* 269–282.

Foa, E. B., Davidson, J.R.T., & Frances, A. (Eds.) (1999). The Expert Consensus Guideline Series: Treatment of Posttraumatic Stress Disorder. *Journal of Clinical Psychiatry, 60* (Suppl. 16), 3–76. .

Farmer, E. M., Compton, S. N., Burns, B. J., & Robertson, E. (2002) Review of the evidence base for treatment of childhood psychopathology: Externalizing disorders. *Journal of Consulting and Clinical Psychology, 70,* 1267–1302.

Fishbein, M., Triandis, H., Kanfer, F., Becker, M., Middlestadt, S., & Eichler, A. (2001). Factors influencing behavior and behavior change. In A. Baum, T. Revenson, & J. Singer (Eds.), *Handbook of health psychology* (pp. 727–746). Mahwah, NJ: Lawrence Erlbaum Associates.

Fristad, M. A., Goldberg-Arnold, J. S., & Gavazzi, S. M. (2003). Multi-family psycho-education groups in the treatment of children with mood disorders. *Journal of Marital and Family Therapy, 29,* 491–504.

Heflinger, C. A., Bickman, L., Northrup, D., & Sonnichsen, S. (1997). A theory-driven intervention and evaluation to explore family caregiver empowerment. *Journal of Emotional and Behavioral Disorders, 5,* 184–191.

Jaccard, J. (1975). A theoretical analysis of selected factors important to health education strategies. *Health Education Monographs, 3,* 152–167.

Jaccard, J., Dodge, T., & Dittus, P. (2002). Parent-adolescent communication about sex and birth control: A conceptual framework. In S. Feldman & D. A. Rosenthal (Eds.), *Talking Sexuality: Parent-Adolescent Communication* (pp.9–41). New Directions for Child and Adolescent Development. Series Editor W. Damon. San Francisco: Jossey-Bass.

Jaccard, J., Litardo, H., & Wan, C. (1999). Subjective culture: Social psychological models of behavior. In J. Adamopoulos & Y. Kashima (Eds.), *Social psychology and cultural context* (pp. 95–106). Newbury Park, CA: Sage.

Jensen, P. (2002) Longer term effects of stimulant treatments for attention deficit/ hyperactivity disorder. *Journal of Attention Disorders, 6*(Suppl. 1), 45–56.

McKay, M., & Bannon, W. (2004). Engaging families in child mental health services. In B. J. Burns & K. E. Hoagwood (Eds.), Evidence-based practice. Part I: Research update. *Child and Adolescent Psychiatric Clinics of North America, 13,* 905–922.

Molina B., for the MTA Cooperative Group. (2007). 36-month substance use and delinquency outcomes in the NIMH MTA. *Journal of the American Academy of Child and Adolescent Psychiatry, 46,* 1027–1039.

MTA Cooperative Group. (1999). A 14-month randomized clinical trial of treatment strategies for attention deficit hyperactivity disorder. *Archives of General Psychiatry, 56,* 1073–1086.

MTA Cooperative Group. (2004). 24-month outcomes of treatment strategies for attention-deficit/hyperactivity disorder (ADHD): The NIMH MTA follow-up. *Pediatrics, 113,* 754–761.

Practice Parameter for the Assessment and Treatment of Children and Adolescents with Anxiety Disorders. (2007). *Journal of the American Academy of Child and Adolescent Psychiatry, 46,* 267–283. Available: www.aacap.org

Ruffolo, M. C. (1998). Mental health services for children and adolescents. In J. B. Williams & K. Ell (Eds.), *Advances in mental health research: Implications for practice* (pp. 399–419). Washington, DC: NASW Press.

Santisteban, D. A., Szapocznik, J., Perez-Vidal, A., Kuartines, W. M., Murray, E. J., & LaPerriere, A. (1996). Efficacy of intervention for engaging youth and families into treatment and some variables that may contribute to differential effectiveness. *Journal of Family Psychology, 10,* 35–44.

Taub, J., Tighe, T. A., & Burchard, J. (2001). The effects of parent empowerment on adjustment for children receiving comprehensive mental health services. *Children's Services: Social Policy, Research, and Practice, 4,* 103–122.

Tcheremissine, O. V., Cherek, D. R., & Lane, S. D. (2004). Psychopharmacology of conduct disorder: Current progress and future directions. *Expert Opinion on Pharmacotherapy, 5,* 1109–1116.

Tuckman, B. (1965). Developmental sequence in small groups. *Psychological Bulletin, 63,* 384–399.

Tuckman, B., & Jensen, M. (1977). Stages of small group development. *Group and Organizational Studies, 2,* 419–427.

U.S. Department of Health and Human Services. (1999). *Mental health: A report of the surgeon general, chapter 3: Children and mental health.* Rockville, MD: U.S. Department of Health and Human Services, Substance Abuse and Mental Health Services Administration, Center for Mental Health Services, National Institutes of Health, National Institute of Mental Health.

U.S. Department of Health and Human Services. (2001). *Mental health: Culture, race, ethnicity—Supplement to Mental health: Report of the surgeon general.* Rockville, MD: U.S. Department of Health and Human Services, Substance Abuse and Mental Health Services Administration, Center for Mental Health Services, National Institutes of Health, National Institute of Mental Health.

Williams, R. J., Chang, S. Y., & Addiction Centre Adolescent Research Group. (2000). A comprehensive and comparative review of adolescent substance abuse treatment outcome. *Clinical Psychology: Science and Practice, 7,* 138–166.

Index